INSTRUCTOR'S RESOURCE GUIDE

to accompany

STRATEGIC MARKET MANAGEMENT

5TH EDITION

DAVID A. AAKER

University of California, Berkeley

Prepared by

DAVID A. AAKER
JIM PROST

University of California, Berkeley

JOHN WILEY & SONS, INC.

NEW YORK • CHICHESTER • WEINHEIM • BRISBANE • SINGAPORE • TORONTO

ISBN 0-471-29789-5

Printed in the United States of America

10 9 8 7 6 5 4 3 2

Printed and bound by Malloy Lithographing, Inc.

INTRODUCTION

INSTRUCTOR'S RESOURCE GUIDE

for *Strategic Market Management*, Fifth Edition
David A. Aaker & Jim Prost

Strategic Market Management can be used in marketing strategy courses at both the undergraduate and graduate levels. These courses can include some combination of cases, readings, projects, papers, and computer simulations such as MARKSTRAT.

Four very different course outlines including the one used at Berkeley are presented in the first section of this guide. The book can also be used in strategy/policy courses in management programs.

- At the University of California, Berkeley, *Strategic Market Management* supports an externally-oriented business strategy course. It has been remarkably well received. About 70% of our 225 second-year MBA students attempt to get into the three sections, which accommodate from 80 to 120 students. A significant number of alumni have said it was their most useful course.
An important objective of the Berkeley course is to provide the students with confidence in their ability to conduct and apply an external analysis. Thus, the first four or five case discussions plus a group project involve a very structured approach to external analysis. Thus, the student emerges with the confidence to conduct an external analysis. Many students have later reported that this skill provided a differential advantage in their first jobs. The course, like the book, also emphasizes the investment decision (enter/grow/milk/exit), how to develop a sustainable competitive advantage, organizational and implementation issues, and global strategic considerations.

The other three course syllabi take very different approaches to the course:

- The Prost course goes through the book sequentially. Each day the class begins with a discussion of one or more current strategic moves that have appeared in the press. It includes a lecture/discussion of the concepts in the chapters and then moves to a case.
- The MARKSTRAT course integrates the MARKSTRAT game into the course.
- The final version uses readings and research papers.

The Instructor Resource Section of this guide contains suggestions as to how an instructor can find examples and stories to support the concepts of the course.

The Lecture Notes Section contains suggestions as to how to create a lecture and discussion around each chapter.

The PowerPoint Section provides supporting presentations. The presentations are designed so that they will also work in black & white.

The Three Cases that appear in this guide were written specifically for this course. The first is a case that was written to support an external analysis of the beer industry. It is positioned as the first case in the course to get students into the subject matter. It allows a focus upon the mechanics of the external analysis. The beer case has been updated with summaries of current readings. The second is the Xerox case written to support Part Three of the book. It illustrates the development of sustainable competitive advantages and how competing firms can overcome them. The Intel case is really a mini-case that allows a full discussion of how to develop and manage a key asset, brand equity. Adopters of the book have permission to reproduce these cases for student use in the class in which the book is adopted.

The final sections are:
A **Test Bank** that includes 200 objective test questions plus 13 essay questions and a description of what is new about the fifth edition.

A **CD-Rom** is attached to this manual that contains an electronic version of the Instructor's Resource Guide, including the Three Cases mentioned with hotlinks to relevant sites on the World Wide Web, and a Test Bank (without the answers). The PowerPoint Presentations are also provided in PowerPoint '95 and '97 versions.

This Instructor's Resource CD-Rom enables instructors to print valuable material for distribution to their students.

In addition, a **Website** has been designed for the book at:
http://www.wiley.com/college/strategic which offers these and other resources for both students and instructors. Whenever possible, **hotlinks** have been provided so that students and instructors can further research the companies and sources mentioned. The **PowerPoint Presentations** can be downloaded in both presentation and notepad format for both instructor presentation and student review.

CONTENTS

INSTRUCTOR'S RESOURCE GUIDE

for *Strategic Market Management*, Fifth Edition

1. Berkeley Case/Project Course Outline   1

2. Prost Discussion/Case/Project Course Outline   13

3. Case/MARKSTRAT Course Outline   21

4. Readings/Paper/Discussion Course Outline   29

5. Cases for Courses using *Strategic Market Management*   33

6. Instructor Resources   39

7. Lecture Notes   47

8. Case: Notes on the Beer Industry   83

9. Teaching Notes: The Beer Industry Case   91

10. Case: Xerox: From the Fifties to the Eighties   99

11. Teaching Notes: Xerox: From the Fifties to the Eighties   115

12. Intel Case   123

13. Teaching Notes: Intel Case   127

14. Test Questions   131

15. Changes in the Fifth Edition of *Strategic Market Management*   159

16. PowerPoint Presentations by Chapter   161

SECTION 1

U.C. BERKELY CASE/PROJECT COURSE OUTLINE

This course is concerned with strategic market management or strategic planning. The focus is on strategic decisions, decisions which have a long-term impact on the organization and which are difficult and costly to reverse. The strategic decision-making process is supported by an external analysis (an analysis of the organization's environment) and an internal analysis. Among the course objectives are to develop the ability to:

1. Conduct the external and internal analyses that support the development of strategies.

2. Identify and address strategic questions such as:
   - What environmental opportunities and threats do we face?
   - What are the key strategic uncertainties?
   - What are our organizational strengths, weaknesses, and problems?
   - What are our strategic alternatives?
   - What business should we be in?
   - What are our long-term objectives, our vision?
   - What product markets are attractive to us?
   - What growth directions are most attractive?
   - How should the organization's resources be allocated?
   - Should we diversify? How?
   - What is our sustainable competitive advantage?
   - What assets or competencies need to be developed and maintained?
   - What should be the strategy with respect to product line, distribution, branding, manufacturing, and finance?

3. Understand and work with a set of useful and important concepts such as unmet needs, strategic groups, sustainable competitive advantage, risk, key success factors, strategic opportunities or threats, strategic strengths, weaknesses, or problems, strategic uncertainties, vision, product markcts, segmentation, industry structure, portfolio analysis, and scenarios.

The course involves case analyses and a group industry report.

Note-- *The assumption is a two-hour class. If this is so, the Hartley case, which normally involves around 20 minutes, is a good supplement to the Harvard case. The Hartley cases allow the student to see more contexts. Shown is a 20-session course that would be suitable for a quarter course meeting twice a week.*

Case Analysis

A large part of the course involves case discussions and the presentation of analyses. It is expected that everyone will prepare the major case of the day in-depth and will discuss it before class with a group of 2 to 6 classmates. The Hartley cases (plus Intel and the branding strategy case) should be read and considered but not analyzed in-depth. Name cards will be used throughout the semester.

Industry Analysis

An industry analysis is to be completed by a team of 3 to 6 people--the groups need not be the same as those used for case analyses but it is usually efficient to have some overlap. To the extent possible, the industry analysis should include:

1. A customer analysis including an identification of the key market segments. Create, if it would be useful, a segment by motivation grid.

2. A market analysis including a market definition, demand trends, product life cycle analysis, and an identification of key success factors.

3. Identification of the important competitors, their strategy objectives, weaknesses, and problems. Attempt to identify the sustainable competitive advantages (SCAs) of each of the major competitors. Were the firms "born" with those SCAs? If not, when and how were they developed? Do any of the firms have a strategic vision?

4. If appropriate, a historical view of the strategies pursued by one, two, or more competitors. Perhaps two competitors can be identified (i.e., Schlitz and Budweiser) who were similar in the '60s but have since pursued very different strategies with different results. Specify what the strategies were, their rationale, and the reason they worked or did not work.

5. If appropriate and feasible, contact one or two operating managers from a firm (or two firms) in the industry. Determine from them:
   - Who is the leading competitor in his/her business;
   - What are the respective sustainable competitive advantages (SCAs), if any, for his/her firm and for the leading competitor;
   - Which of the SCAs the involved firms were "born" with and which they "developed."

6. An analysis of the major environmental trends, opportunities, and threats. Consider doing a scenario analysis. Develop one or two alternative scenarios different from base line assumptions. The scenario could be the accentuation of a trend or the occurrence of a future event, or it could be motivated by a strategic uncertainty. For that (or those) scenario(s), address the following questions:
   - What causal factors will influence whether the scenario emerges?
   - What are the implications for external analysis--segments, motivations, competitors, industrial structure, key success factors, etc.?
   - What strategies would be optimal?

7. An assessment of the industry in terms of the GE "industry attractiveness" dimension and the BCG "market growth" dimension.

8. The completion of a "planning form" as illustrated in the text appendix.

9. Finally, put yourself in the position of an adviser for one or more of the competitors and assess the strategic alternatives. Or assume your client is someone considering entering the market. What entry alternatives would you consider? At the outset of the report (both oral and written) it will be helpful to indicate the client and the nature of strategic decisions the client is (or should be) facing if such decisions can be identified. The identification of a client will help you determine the strategically important material and avoid getting overwhelmed by information and becoming too descriptive.

An industry should be selected for which information is available in trade magazines and business publications like *Business Week* and *Fortune*. Possible industries include gourmet frozen foods, wine, retail banking, a software area, soda pop, frozen novelties, department stores, fiber optics, food retailing, a type of restaurant, automobiles, cross-country skis, drug equipment, personal computers, tennis equipment, etc.

Please hand in by September 30, but earlier if possible, a report which lists:
   1. Group members
   2. The industry and client selected
   3. A preliminary list of
      -strategic uncertainties
      -strategic decision options the your client is likely to face

The report (both oral and written) is due December 2 - the last day of class - and should be as concise as possible. Free use should be made of appendices for

3

descriptive background material. However, material that is worth discussing and supports strategic insights and recommendations should appear in the body and/or as figures. To the extent possible, the report should go beyond descriptive material to get at strategic implications. It is helpful if the paper starts with an introduction that briefly describes the client, sets forth the objectives of the study, motivates the project, and provides an overview of the paper structure. It is very helpful to provide a feel for the strategic problems and alternatives facing the client. This should be used to motivate and provide implications in the body of the report. An executive summary is not required and, if included, should not take the place of an introductory section. It is not imperative that the group agree upon the interpretation and conclusions. A note setting forth areas of disagreement is appropriate if a group member has an opinion not shared by others.

In both the written and oral report, do not attempt to be comprehensive when covering a section like competitor analysis--just discuss those areas that add insight. The goal is to be insightful and helpful to the client--not to cover every dimension of the external analysis. Introduce strategic questions, threats, opportunities, and judgments about strategic options as you go along. Do not save them for the end. The recommendation section can then be a summary of the questions and options that have already been raised and discussed in the context of the analysis. One goal should be to create a link between the external analysis and the recommendations. You should consider defending and justifying each summary recommendation with respect to the rationale, effort/cost, and risks involved. If more information is needed, it might be worthwhile to set forth how it might be obtained and what will be done with it.

In addition to the paper, there will be a 25 minute presentation of the findings. This presentation should be polished, professional, rehearsed (using the videotape facility if possible), interesting, punchy, and useful to your client. You should regard it as an excellent opportunity to improve or refine your presentation skills. Everyone should present, although if there is a large group, someone who is extremely skilled at presentation can be excluded.

During the presentation of the other groups, you will be asked provide written comments on the presentation skills of each speaker (not the content) and what suggestions for improvement you would make. A set of these comments will be copied (with the author's name excluded) and returned to you on the last day of class. The goal is not only to provide feedback but also to sensitize you to presentation skills.

Executive Presentations

The plan is to arrange for an executive to speak on a Monday afternoon. Assuming it works out, this lecture will become a part of the course, and all students are expected to attend. There will be a sign-up sheet that you should be sure to sign.

Final

There may be a take-home final examination.

Industry Interview

1. Contact an operating manager and determine:
   a) Who is the leading competitor in his/her business.
   b) What are the respective sustainable competitive advantages (SCAs), if any, for his/her firm and for the leading competitors.
   c) Which of the SCAs the involved firms were "born" with and which they "developed."
   d) Whether any of the competitors operated with a clear strategic vision. If so has this vision been helpful?

Grade

Case work will count toward about 60% of the grade. The case work grade will be primarily based upon class participation but will also include participation in case-study groups. The industry report will be worth around 40%. Members of the group may receive different grades based upon their oral presentation, their section in the report (if it is well defined), and their role in the group. At the end of the course, each student will be given the chance to describe the role played by each of the members of his or her case discussion and/or industry analysis group. Who did what in terms of organizing, leading discussions, sections, writing, etc.? Of particular interest is learning about excellent performance that may not have been reflected completely in class or in the group oral or written report.

Texts

Aaker, David A., Strategic Market Management, 5th Edition, John Wiley & Sons, 1999. In the course readings, the numbers refer to chapters in this book.

Hartley, Robert F., Marketing Mistakes, John Wiley & Sons, 7th Edition, 1998.
    For the Hartley cases ask:
            What happened and why? What would you have done differently?

Course Outline	**Readings**
1. External and Internal Analysis	1 ,2, 3, 4, 5, 6, 7, 16
2. Corporation Strengths & Synergies	7, 8, 9, 10, 11, 14
a. Consider Intel and Osborne.	Intel Case (in this teacher's guide) Hartley: Osborne
b. What is the strength of Weight Watchers?	The Weight Watchers Story from <u>Managing</u> <u>Brand Equity</u>
c. What should they do in the face of the Healthy Choice brand and the change in eating habits it represents?	
d. What would you say are the strengths of Nike?	"High Performance Marketing"
e. Why can Nike support so many brands (i.e. Basketball--Force, Flight, Air Jordan)?	(*HBR* July-Aug, 1992)

The Strategic Analysis

3. The Beer Industry	Notes on the Beer Industry; Review 3,4,5,6 Hartley: Snapple
a. Conduct a complete external analysis of the beer industry.	
b. What are the important threats, opportunities, trends, and strategic uncertainties? What are the implications for Miller's?	
c. What do you see as the strategy alternatives for Miller's?	
d. Read the Snapple case from Hartley.	

4. International Systems: A Growth Industry

    a. Conduct an external/internal analysis.

    b. Identify key threats, opportunities, trends and strategic uncertainties.

    c. Should IS enter the CT scanner industry? If so, what entry strategy would you pursue? What investment strategy

should they pursue with respect to the
X-ray business?

d. What would you do if you were in GE's
shoes?

5. Kunz: A Declining Industry

13, Review 11,12
Hartley: McDonald's

a. Conduct an external/internal analysis.
b. Evaluate the strategic alternatives.
c. How much would you pay for Kunz?
Be prepared to defend your price.

6. Apple Computer 1992

Hartley: IBM

a. Conduct an external/internal analysis.
b. Does Apple need to change the structure of the
personal computer industry in 1992 to retain its
competitive advantage? Why/Why not?
c. Evaluate Apple's strategy since 1990; how will it
affect Apple's competitive position and the structure
of the industry?
d. What should Sculley do in 1992?

7. Crown Cork & Seal

Review 12
Hartley: Borden

a. Conduct an external/internal analysis.
b. What is your assessment of the
industry?
c. Why has Crown succeeded?
d. What should Crown do now?

The Sustainable Competitive Advantage

8. Xerox

Review 8
Hartley: Euro Disney

a. Identify and evaluate Xerox strategy
in the 1960's.
b. What entry barriers did Xerox create
in the 1960's?
c. Identify and evaluate the strategy
of IBM, Kodak, Ricoh/Savin, Canon, and
Minolta. How did each overcome Xerox's

entry barriers?

    d. Why did Xerox lose position in the 1970's?

    e. What were the strengths and weaknesses of Xerox in 1980?

    f. What should Xerox do to come back in the 1980's?

9. Wal-Mart Stores' Discount Operations   Hartley: Sears

    a. How do you explain Wal-Mart's extraordinary performance in discount retailing?

    b. How sustainable is Wal-Mart's competitive advantage in discount retailing in 1986?

    c. What do you think of Wal-Mart's diversification in Sam's Wholesale Clubs?

10. Asahi Breweries   15
                                                     Hartley: Coca Cola

    a. Consider the 1947-1980 period. How did Kirin gain and keep such a dominant position? How did Asahi compete during that period? Why didn't their innovations result in SCAs?

    b. What was Asahi's position in 1980? If you were made CEO how would you revive the firm? What did Murai do? Were those actions critical to the success of Asahi?

    c. Who is the better CEO: Murai or Higuchi?

    d. What is the SCA of Asahi?

    f. The new expansion play--Go or no-go?

    g. What is the expected response of competitors?

11. Bayerische Motoren Werke AG (BMW)   Hartley: Harley-
                                                            Davidson

    a. What was BMW's status in the market in 1986? Who was buying BMW and what were they buying?

b. Conduct an external analysis as of 1991. What are the major trends, strategic questions, and threats facing BMW?

c. What caused the unit sales decline from 1986-1991? Could BMW have prevented it given its position in 1986?

d. Evaluate Gerlinger's performance. What has he accomplished to date? Can BMW effectively compete against Lexus and Infiniti?

e. What advice would you give Gerlinger to help him achieve his 100,000 unit sales goal?

12. Saatchi & Saatchi

a. What was the S&S source of success in the 1970s?

b. What was the S&S acquisition strategy in the 1970s and early 1980s? Evaluate it.

c. Evaluate the concept of the conglomerate agency and the decision by S&S to have two of them. What types of communication companies are included? What synergies are expected? For what customer problems is this a solution? What are the problems of managing a communication conglomerate? How could you make it work and overcome these problems? What other solutions are there to these problems?

d. Would you say that having a global presence is a key success factor? Why? If you were Budweiser would you want a global agency? Why? What are the advantages and disadvantages? How can you organize it to make it work?

e. Why didn't the US agencies exploit their size and skills to dominate world wide advertising in the 1980s? Why didn't Japanese agencies dominate advertising like they did banking?

13. Grand Metropolitan   7,8
                                                Hartley: Southwest
Airlines

a. Conduct an internal analysis.

b. What are Grand Met's strengths? Is branding a strength? Why?

9

c. What is its vision?
d. Will it succeed?
e. What would you do differently?

14. Benetton   Hartley: Microsoft

a. What are the SCAs of Benetton?
b. Which elements of strategy and
   SCAs can Benetton maintain in the US
   market?
c. Would you introduce Benetton into the
   US at the time of the case? Why and
   how or why not?
d. As Mr. Aluffi and Mr. Palmeri,
   what would you do first? Second? Third?
e. How would you resolve the questions
   posed in the case? Are these the right
   questions to address?

15. MCI Telecommunications Corp (A)

a. In 1981 is MCI a successful company?
b. What factors have made MCI able to
   compete so successfully in the
   long distance market against AT&T and
   also against Southern Pacific and U.S.
   Transmission Systems?
c. What role has marketing played in
   the company's success?
   How has the marketing function and
   organization changed over time?
d. As of 1981 what do you see as the
   principal risks facing MCI? How would
   you deal with them.

16. The Sustainable Competitive Advantage   8, 9, 10

a. Be prepared to discuss your   Hartley: Saturn
   industry interview

The Exit Decision

17. EG&G. A&B   13, 15

    a. What should Freed do about the   Hartley: Nike
       Electro-Mechanical Division?
    b. Should it be divested?
    c. How should Freed handle the
       upcoming meeting?
    d. Critique the planning forms.

18. Industry Reports

19. Industry Reports

20. Summary--Wrap-up.
    Reports due

Reminder--This outline assumes two-hour class sessions.

SECTION 2

PROST DISCUSSION/CASE/PROJECT COURSE OUTLINE

This is the outline for the course created and taught by Jim Prost, who also created the Lecture Notes, PowerPoint Presentation, and Instructor Resource sections for this Instructor Resource Guide.

The outline begins on the next page.

STRATEGIC MARKETING

Course Outline

Reading assignments are to be completed prior to and in preparation for class discussion. They are critical to the success of the course and to your comprehension of marketing strategies. Assignments are subject to change as may become appropriate. The material for **ASSIGNMENTS** are found in the following books: *Chapters* are found in **Strategic Market Management** (5th edition) by David Aaker; *Cases* are found in **Strategic Marketing Management Cases** (5th edition) by Cravens, Lamb and Crittenden; *Articles* will be handed out in class.

DATE	TOPIC(S)	ASSIGNMENTS
February 17 Tuesday	**Introduction and Overview** Introduction to Strategic Marketing; Review of the Marketing Mix; The Strategic Triangle; Why strategic marketing is important, its role and value in marketing management to achieve a sustainable competitive advantage. The strategic implications for creative and critical thinking in strategy formulation.	Chapters: 1 & 2 and Case Book: Appendix B *Guide to Marketing Case Analysis* (pages 701-714) Case: *Coca-Cola (Japan) Company* Article: *What the Hell is "Market Oriented"?*
February 24 Tuesday	**Strategic Market Management** What is a Business Strategy? Strategic Thrusts and SCAs; Why Strategic Market Management; Characteristics and Trends; External Analysis and Internal Analysis.	
March 3 Tuesday	**External Analysis** The Scope of Customer Analysis; Segmentation; Customer Motivations	Chapter 3
	Competitor Analysis Identifying Competitors; Potential Competitors; Competitor Analysis	Chapter 4 ❶ Case: *The Metropolitan Museum of Art* Article: *The Fall and Rise of Strategic Planning*

14

March 10
Tuesday

Market Analysis
Dimensions of Market Analysis; Market Growth; Cost Structure; Distribution Systems; Key Success Factors.

Chapter 5

Environmental Analysis and Dealing with Strategic Uncertainty
Dimensions of Environmental Analysis; Scenario Analysis, Forecasting Environmental Trends and Events.

Chapter 6
❷ Case: *Blockbuster Entertainment Corp.*

March 17
Tuesday

Midterm Exam

Internal Analysis
Shareholder Value Analysis; Determinants of Strategic Options; From Analysis to Strategy; Business Portfolio Analysis.

Chapter 7
❸ Case: *LoJack Corp.*
Article: *The Core Competence of the Corporation*

March 24
Tuesday

Obtaining A Sustainable Competitive Advantage
The Sustainable Competitive Advantage; The Role of Synergy; Strategic Vision versus Strategic Opportunism; Strategic Intent.

Chapter 8
Article: *Strategic Intent*
❹ Case: *The North Face*

Differentiation Strategies
Successful Differentiation Strategies; The Quality Option; Building Strong Brands

Chapter 9
❺ Case: *TenderCare Disposable Diapers Corp.*

Obtaining an SCA: Low Cost, Focus, and the Preemptive Move
Low-Cost Strategies; The Experience Curve; Focus Strategies; The Preemptive Move; Follower Advantages.

Chapter 10
Article: *Sustainable Advantage*

March 31
Tuesday

Growth Strategies: Penetration, Product-Market Expansion, and Vertical Integration
Growth in Existing Product Markets; Product Development for the Existing Market; Market Development Using Existing Products; Vertical Integration Strategies.

Chapter 11
❻ Case: *Rollerblade, Inc.,*

Diversification
Related Diversification; Unrelated Diversification; Entry Strategies

Chapter 12

Strategies in Declining and Mature Markets
Creating Growth in Declining Industries; Be the Profitable Survivor; Milk or Harvest; Divestment or Liquidation; Selecting the Right Strategy for the Declining Environment; Hostile Markets.

Chapter 13
Article: *What is Strategy?*

April 7
Tuesday

Global Strategies
Motivations Underlying Global Strategies; Standardization versus Customization; Strategic Alliances.

Chapter 14

Implementing the Strategy
A Conceptual Framework; Structure; Systems; People; Culture; Obtaining Strategic Congruence; Organizing for Innovation.

Chapter 15
❼ Case: *Yoplait USA*

Formal Planning Systems
Pitfalls of a Formal Planning System.

Chapter 16

April 14
Tuesday

Final Exam

Strategic Market Analysis Presentations
Student teams make formal presentations of a strategic market analysis with recommendations, supporting arguments, and conclusions drawn from their own investigation.

Required Texts:

Strategic Market Management, 5th Edition
Author: David A. Aaker
Publisher: John Wiley & Sons, 1999

Strategic Marketing Management Cases, 5th Edition
Authors: Cravens, Lamb and Crittenden
Publisher: Irwin, 1996

16

STRATEGIC MARKETING

Spring 1998

GROUP PRESENTATIONS

DATE	CASE	PRESENTATION	BOARD OF DIRECTORS
March 3 **Tuesday**	*The Metropolitan Museum of Art*	Group 1	Group 5
March 10 **Tuesday**	*Blockbuster Entertainment Corp.*	Group 2	Group 6
March 17 **Tuesday**	*LoJack Corporation*	Group 3	Group 7
March 24 **Tuesday**	*The North Face*	Group 4	Group 1
March 24 **Tuesday**	*TenderCare Disposable Diapers*	Group 5	Group 2
March 31 **Tuesday**	*Rollerblade, Inc.*	Group 6	Group 3
April 7 **Tuesday**	*Yoplait USA*	Group 7	Group 4

17

GROUP 1	GROUP 2	GROUP 3	GROUP 4	GROUP 5	GROUP 6	GROUP 7
_____	_____	_____	_____	_____	_____	_____
_____	_____	_____	_____	_____	_____	_____
_____	_____	_____	_____	_____	_____	_____
_____	_____	_____	_____	_____	_____	_____
_____	_____	_____	_____	_____	_____	_____

PRESENTATION GROUP

Your group will prepare a written case analysis, 9 – 12 pages in length, typewritten and double-spaced. The analysis is to be submitted prior to the group's presentation to the class. Each student will receive a grade based on the written case analysis and an individual grade based on his or her presentation in class. All students are expected to present in class. Areas of interest will be organization, presentation skills, and marketing strategies presented.

BOARD OF DIRECTORS GROUP

Each group will act as a Board of Directors to a Case Presentation. Your objective will be to determine if the Presentation Group has convinced you that their strategies were well founded and that their recommendations will achieve the marketing expectations of the case. The Board of Directors is to submit (prior to the Presentation Group's oral presentation) a list of issues they expect to be answered by the Presentation Group.

<u>Final Project Instructions</u>

Each group will select a company from a list provided during class. The group is to prepare an analysis of that company and a **20** minute presentation that the group will present to the class during the last two classes. Each individual will receive a grade based on the group report and on their individual class presentation. The analysis should be typewritten, double-spaced, spell-checked and be 10-14 pages in length. (Pictures, graphs, and supporting documents will be in addition to the 10-14 page limit.)

Please address the following issues:

1)   The type of organization and overall goals of that organization.

2)   The competitive situation in which the company operates.

3)   The organization's target market (in terms of demographics, psychographics, and other characteristics).

4)   The organization's product and/or service attributes and positioning strategy.

5)   What are the key success factors for this market? Does your company have a sustainable competitive advantage? What components provide the SCA?

6)   Promotional activities the companies uses to get and keep their customers.

7)   An assessment of strengths, weaknesses, and effectiveness of the organization's marketing strategy, along with recommendations for improvements or modifications.

Be creative and have fun!

STRATEGIC MARKETING

Spring 1998

Final Project Companies

<u>COMPANY</u>	<u>GROUP</u>
Starbucks	_____
American Cancer Society	_____
Compaq Computer Corporation	_____
Levi Strauss & Co.	_____
FAO Schwartz	_____
Saturn Car Company	_____
Crystal Geyser Water	_____
Nordstrom	_____
Kendall-Jackson Winery	_____
Pea Pod	_____
Coca Cola	_____
Snapple	_____
Southwest Airlines	_____
Citicorp	_____
The Gap	_____
Clorox	_____
Gallo Wines	_____

SECTION 3

CASE/MARKSTRAT COURSE OUTLINE

Course Description

The purpose of this course is to develop an understanding of and skill and experience in formulating and planning marketing strategies. The focus of the course is decidedly <u>strategic</u>. The central focus is on designing strategies for various stages in the product life cycle, including strategies for entry, growth, and defending a brand's position. Tactical elements of marketing receive much less attention, although discussion of them plays an important role in one unit of the course.

The course material consists of a mix of lectures, cases, and a computer-simulation game, MARKSTRAT. The lectures summarize the theory of strategic marketing, drawing heavily on research in marketing and relevant work in management science and economics. Topics include competitive analysis and decision-making, industry analysis, and models of competition and strategy. Cases and computer simulations follow the lectures, illustrating both the theory and its application, in addition to giving students actual experience in formulating competitive strategies. MARKSTRAT is especially useful for this because students make a number of decisions over the entire semester, competing against other members of the class.

Course Requirements

Evaluation of student performance will be based on class participation and case memos (30%), three management reports (20%), and performance in the MARKSTRAT game and the final strategic marketing plan (50%).

Study Groups

Forming study groups is required. All written assignments related to the game in addition to the MARKSTRAT simulation are to be completed in these groups. Actual group size will depend on class enrollment. A deadline for forming study groups will be announced in class.

Class Discussion

A significant portion of the course material is presented in lectures and case discussions. Your consistent involvement in these classes is essential to achieving the objectives of the course. So unless you are willing to arrive on time, prepared for discussion and planning to stay for the entire class, don't come at all.

Case Analyses

For most cases, you will be required to submit a brief memo prepared individually outlining your recommendations. Specific assignments for each case appear on the syllabus. These case memos are to be handed in at the start of class on the day due, and will be graded. Late memos will not be accepted.

MARKSTRAT Simulation

Each team will be assigned a MARKSTRAT firm. Your task will be to (1) set marketing and financial objectives, (2) develop strategies to achieve those objectives, and (3) implement those strategies with appropriate tactical decisions.

You will be required to report periodically on your assessment of your firm, its competitors, and your strategies. In all, three management reports will be required. Each of these three reports should not exceed three double-spaced typewritten pages (plus tables and appendices). Deadlines for their submission are noted on the outline. Late papers will not be accepted.

1. Competitive Marketing Analysis. First, assess your initial market position (including your products, competitors, and potential for growth). In doing so, answer these questions: What are the principal strengths and weaknesses of the firm and its starting position? What is the best possible competitive position for your firm? And, how do buyer preferences vary throughout the market? Second, complete a similar analysis for each competitor to suggest an appropriate business definition for each firm.

2. Initial Strategy. Provide a clear statement of your objectives, your strategy for achieving those objectives, and the tactics you plan to use to implement your strategies. Present strong evidence that your objectives, strategies, and tactics are consistent with your business definition and that they are the best available alternatives.

3. Growth Strategy/Strategy Update. Provide a clear statement of your strategy for growth and update your initial strategy. As in that second paper, present

convincing evidence that your objectives, strategies, and tactics are consistent and that they are the best available alternatives.

Strategic Marketing Plan

In place of a final exam, a final report is required. Your report should detail:

1. Your objectives, strategies, and tactics employed during MARKSTRAT. Include a clear statement of your business definition.

2. A statement of the current market conditions including (i) a profile of buyer preferences and trends, (ii) an analysis of industry trends, (iii) a statement of competitor strengths and weaknesses and anticipated competitor actions, and (iv) a frank assessment of your firm's strengths and weaknesses.

3. A strategic, market-oriented plan for the next five periods. This should include (i) a clear statement of your planned business definition, (ii) marketing and financial objectives in some detail including a specific time-table, (iii) an overall strategy for achieving stated objectives, and (iv) tactics for implementing your strategy accompanied by detailed timetables, budgets, and projected performance for the planning period.

The final strategic plan should not exceed ten double-spaced typed pages (plus tables and appendices). Be sure to summarize the strategic picture. Final reports will be presented during last class, followed by an industry "debriefing".

Course Administration

Office hours are 1:00 - 2:00 Monday and Wednesday. Additional times set aside for MARKSTRAT consultation (i.e., specific MARKSTRAT questions or negotiations) are noted on the outline. All office hours are strictly enforced. If you cannot see me during these times, please make an appointment.

Texts

Aaker, Strategic Market Management, 5th Ed. (Wiley, 1999).
Larrache and Gatignon, MARKSTRAT: A Strategic Marketing Game, (Scientific Press, 1977).
A case packet.
A readings packet.

Course Outline

Session 1:   CONCEPTS OF STRATEGIC MARKETING

Aaker, <u>Strategic Market Management</u>, Chs. 1, 2.

Session 2:   CONCEPTS OF STRATEGIC MARKETING (cont'd)

Aaker, <u>Strategic Market Management</u>, Chs. 3, 4, 5, 6, 7,
 15, 16.

Session 3:   INTRODUCTION TO MARKSTRAT

Larrache and Gatignon, <u>MARKSTRAT: A Strategic Marketing
     Game</u>.

Session 4:   MARKETING STRATEGIES FOR ENTRY I

Aaker, <u>Strategic Market Management</u>, Chs. 8, 9, 10.

Carpenter, "Market Pioneering and Competitive
     Positioning Strategies," <u>Annales de Telecommuni-
     cations</u>, November 1987.

Session 5:   MARKETING STRATEGIES FOR ENTRY II

Aaker, <u>Strategic Market Management</u>, Chs. 11, 12.

Case: Wilmington Corporation (9-576-197)

<u>Assignment</u>:

In a one-page memo, outline the strategic alternatives faced by the
Wilmington Consumer Products Division in the glass-ceramic
cookware market. Be prepared to defend your choice.

Session 6:   MARKETING STRATEGIES FOR ENTRY III

Case: Amicon Corp. (A) (9-579-093)

Assignment:

Discuss the trade-offs involved among the various entry options being considered by Amicon-- direct entry, joint venture, and licensing. Suggest which option they should select, and why, and discuss implementation of it.

Aaker, Strategic Market Management, Ch. 14.

Session 7:   MARKSTRAT DECISION I

Decision due 3:20 PM.
Competitor Marketing Analysis due.

Session 8:   DEFENSIVE MARKETING STRATEGIES I

Hauser, "Theory and Application of Defensive Strategy" in L.G. Thomas (ed.) The Economics of Strategic Planning (Lexington, MA: Lexington Books, 1986).

Session 9:   MARKSTRAT DECISION II

Decision due 3:20 PM.

Session 10:   DEFENSIVE MARKETING STRATEGIES II

Case: Sealed Air Corporation (9-582-103)

Assignment:

In a brief one-page memo, present Sealed Air's possible responses to its new competition. Consider these alternatives and recommend one to Mr. Hauser, along with brief remarks on implementation.

Session 11:   MARKSTRAT DECISION III

Decision due 3:20 PM.

Initial strategy memo due 3:20 PM.

Session 12: DEFENSIVE MARKETING STRATEGIES III

Case: Pepsi Cola U.K. (A) (9-584-052)

Assignment:

Analyze the impending launch of Diet Coke in the U.K. and its implications for Pepsi. In particular, consider Coke's short- and long-term impact on Pepsi in both the U.K. and the U.S. Suggest an appropriate defensive strategy for Pepsi. Present and support your analysis and recommendation in a one-page memo.

Session 13: MARKSTRAT DECISION IV

Decision due 3:20 PM.

Session 14: MARKETING STRATEGIES FOR GROWTH I

Aaker, Strategic Market Management, Chs. 11-12.

MacMillan, "Preemptive Strategies."

MacMillan, "Guerrilla Warfare," Journal of Business Strategy.

Session 15: MARKSTRAT DECISION V

Decision due 3:20 PM.

Session 16: MARKETING STRAGIES FOR GROWTH II
Case: EMI and CT Scanner (B) (9-383-195)
Assignment:

In a one-page memo, outline the current threats and opportunities facing EMI in the CAT scanner market. Discuss EMI's current position, and recommend a strategy for growth.

Session 17: MARKSTRAT DECISION VI

Decision due 3:20 PM.

Growth Strategy memo due 3:20 PM.

Session 18:   MARKETING STRATEGIES FOR GROWTH III

Case: Poland Springs Bottling Corp. (9-580-108)

Assignment:

Analyze the bottled water market and Poland Spring's position to suggest a growth strategy. Be sure to consider the competitive positioning of brands. Summarize your analysis and recommendations in a one-page memo.

Session 19:   MARKSTRAT DECISION VII

Decision due 3:20 PM.

Session 20:   MARKETING STRATEGIES FOR MATURE BRANDS I

Aaker, Strategic Market Management, Ch. 13

Hammermesh and Silk, "How to compete in stagnant industries," Harvard Business Review, Sept.-Oct. 1979

Session 21:   MARKSTRAT DECISION VIII

Decision due 3:20 PM.

Session 22:   MARKETING STRATEGIES FOR MATURE AND DECLINING BRANDS II

Case: U.S. Retail Coffee Market (A) (9-582-087)

Assignment:

1. Make and justify the following forecasts:

a. the size of the total retail market in F'83 and F'88.

b. the split of the market by major segments for F'83 and F'88.

2. What are the implications of your forecasts for the marketing strategy of each major producer?

Summarize your work in a brief two-page memo to be handed in at <u>the start of class</u>.

Aaker, <u>Strategic Market Management</u>, Ch. 10.

Session 23:   MARKETING STRATEGIES FOR MATURE AND DECLINING BRANDS III

Case: U.S. Retail Coffee Market (B) and Brim (A)
      (9-582-088; 9-582-099)

<u>Assignment</u>:

In a brief two-page memo, summarize your thoughts on the following issues:

1. Assess Maxwell House Division's situation in 1978.

2. What should GF do about MHD?

3. What will P & G and Nestle do?

4. Assess Brim's situation in 1978.

5. What should MHD do about Brim?

6. What will Brim's competitors do?

Session 24:   MARKSTRAT PRESENTATIONS AND DEBRIEFING

READINGS/PAPER/DISCUSSION COURSE OUTLINE

Objective

The major objective of this seminar is to provide students with the opportunity to discuss emerging issues in marketing particularly as they influence marketing strategy. Contemporary writings in marketing strategy will be focused on in the seminar. Emphasis of the discussion shall be upon analyzing the validity of the authors' observations and examining the value they hold for the practicing manager. Particular concern will also be given to issues stemming from the external and competitive environment which impact marketing decisions. There will be weekly assignments as well as a major term paper.

Required Texts and Materials

D.A. Aaker, Strategic Market Management, 5th Edition, (New York: John Wiley and Sons, 1999).

A current marketing strategy readings book

Selected articles (to be handed out)

Absences

Because the experience of this seminar requires the intense preparation and participation of seminar members for each session, no more than one class absence will be permitted. If personal or job requirements are expected to necessitate absence in excess of one class meeting, enrollment is not recommended.

Class Format

Each class will generally follow the following format:

o First 20 minutes: general discussion and housekeeping. Students are strongly encouraged to bring up questions or make comments concerning articles dealing with marketing which they have read in business periodicals (<u>Business Week</u>, <u>Fortune</u>, <u>WSJ</u>) or the general press. This module provides an opportunity to address the most recent developments in marketing practice. Questions stemming from the marketing dimensions of one's own job situation are also appropriate.

o   Next 50 minutes: discussion of special handouts, textbook chapter(s) assigned and any instructor presentation.

o   Break: 10 minutes

o   Last 70 minutes: discussion of articles assigned from reader and/or handouts.

(Student responsibilities involve the submission of a two or three page outline for each article [typed or neatly handwritten] which summarizes the key points and responds to the inquiries posed in the weekly assignment sheet.)

The overriding goal of the seminar is for the class to develop propositions and principles about strategy from the original sources while maintaining an ability to be critical about the validity of the propositions.

Major Paper Assignment

Prepare a 12-15-page typewritten paper (exclusive of exhibits, tables and references) which describes and analyzes the marketing strategy used by a specific company or industry. Analysis should be conducted at the Strategic Business Unit level. The strategy should be analyzed in terms of the readings which have been discussed. Examples of paper topics which might be acceptable:

o   the marketing of construction equipment in developing nations by John Deere;

o   how Apple has attacked the business market;

o   the marketing of BMW's in the U.S.;

o   an analysis of the automated machine tool industry in Europe;

o   the success of Coors in the face of a mature beer industry and aggressive large competitors.

Thus, the purpose of the exercise is to clinically describe a marketing campaign and then evaluate it in terms of the axioms of marketing strategy.
In any event, ALL TOPICS SHOULD BE CLEARED IN ADVANCE with the instructor. Technical aspects of the paper should follow the style of the <u>Journal of Marketing</u>. Other technical questions are referred to: K.L. Turabian, <u>A Manual for Writers of Term Papers, Thesis and Dissertations</u> (Current Edition), University of Chicago Press.

Course Assessment Scheme

Class Outlines	20%	(see below)
Class Discussion	30%	
Term Paper	50%	

Preparation for Discussion and Outline Format
(Weekly Assignment):

In addition to summarizing the major points of the articles, each reading outline should answer the following questions:

1.   What is the major theme of this article?

2.   Is the author's message valid in today's environment for the practicing manager? For your organization?

3.   What criticisms do you have of the author's methods and arguments?

4.   What implications does this article suggest for the conduct of marketing?

ASSIGNMENTS

Session	Aaker (Chapters)	Readings Book (Article Nos.)	Article Handouts
1. Introduction	1,2,	16	Levitt
2. External Analysis	3,4,5,6	8, 12	
3. Information Technology Market Share Experience Curve			
5. (*) [SELECTION OF TERM PAPER TOPIC IS DUE]			
6. Segmentation			
7. Positioning			
8. Strategic Vision			
.			
.			
.			
.			
.			
.			
13. (*) PAPER PREPARATION; INSTRUCTOR/STUDENT CONSULTATION			
14. PAPER DUE; PAPER PRESENTATIONS			
15. PAPER PRESENTATIONS/ CLASS SUMMARY			

SECTION 5

CASES FOR COURSES USING <u>STRATEGIC MARKET MANAGEMENT</u>.

Note: The numbers shown in parentheses are the Harvard case numbers. A "TN" indicates a teacher's note.

New Cases
The Charles Schwab Corporation in 1996 (SM35)
Note on the consumer on-line Services Industry (SM33)
R.R. Donnelley & Sons and Digital Technology 1995-1997 (SM43)
Dewar's (A): Brand Repositioning in 1990s (9-596-076)
Eastman Kodak Co.: Funtime Film (9-594-111) (TN5-597-080)
Egon Zehnder International (9-398-059)
Executone Information Systems, Inc. (9-793-140) (TN 5-794-040)
Loblaw Companies Ltd.: Food Distribution in the1990s (9-593-033)
Philip Morris: Marlboro Friday (9-596-001) (Supplement 9-596-002)
TV Guide (9-395-032) (TN 5-396-252)

From Outline 1
Intel Case (Reproduced in this resource guide)
Notes on the Beer Industry (Reproduced in this resource guide)
International Systems: CT Scanner (9-578-182)
Kunz (9-577-115)--out of print
Apple Computer 1992 (9-792-081)
Crown Cork & Seal (9-378-024) (TN 5-378-108)
Xerox (Reproduced in this resource guide)
Wal-Mart Stores' Discount Operations (9-387-018) (TN 5-387-127)
Asahi Breweries (9-389-114) (TN 5-389-213)
Bayerische Motoren Werke AB (BMW) (9-593-082) (TN50594-107)
Saatchi & Saatchi (9-792-056)
Grand Metropolitan (9-590-056)
Benetton (A) 9-685-014 (TN 5-686-019)
MCI Telecommunications Corp (A) (9-582-106) (TN 5-584-057)
EG&G (9-377-027; 9-376-188) (TN 5-377-028)

From Outline 3
Wilmington Corp. (9-576-197)
Amicon Corp. (A) (9-569-093)
Sealed Air Corporation (9-582-103)
Pepsi Cola U.K. (9-584-052)

EMI and CT SCANNER (B) (9-383-195) (TN 5-384-030)
Poland Springs Bottling Corp. (9-580-108)
U.S. Retail Coffee Market (A) (9-582-087) (TN 5-585-108)
Brim (A) (9-582-099)

Other Course Outlines

Caterpillar (9-385-276) (Supp--9-387-195) (TN 5-388-129)
Komatsu ((9-385-277) (Supp--9-387-095) (TN 5-388-130)
      Charts two very different strategies.
General Electric: Clock and Timer Market Strategy (9-582-031;9-582-151) (TN 5-585-009)
      -On applying portfolio analysis.
Hewlett-Packard: Manufacturing Productivity Division (A) (0-587-101)
      -On integrating functional area strategies including marketing, R&D, and
       product support.
Hewlett-Packard: Manufacturing Productivity Division (B) (0-587-102)
      -Issues of organizational structure and how they interact with strategy.
Robert Mondavi Winery (1-583-036)
      -Issues of globalization and obtaining supply and marketing.
CompuServe (A) (9-386-067) (TN 5-386-086)
      -Resources needed to support needed strategic moves are limited.
      -Relationships with parent H&R Block considered.
Polo Fashions: Ralph Lauren Womenswear, Inc., (0-586-058)
      -Segmentation of the fashion industry, firm's strengths and weaknesses,
       role of the distribution system in strategy
Applied Materials, Inc. (0-585-003)
      -The role of post sale service and support
British Airways, (9-585-014)
      -Globalization of the advertising function.
Applicon, Inc: National Accounts Program (9-582-010) (TN 5-583-141)
      -Excellent case on implementation to go with Chapter 16. Problems
       associated with a national accounts program and the need to develop a
       supporting sales support program.
Water Meter Industry in 1982 (9-386-128)
      -The competitive situation facing Rockwell, the market leader of an
       industry undergoing structural change. Whether or not to add a plastic
       case meter on the market is one visible option.
General Electric: Strategic Position--1981 (9-381-174) (TN 5-385-089)
      -Describes Reg Jones tenure as CEO of GE.
General Electric--1984 (9-385-315)
      -The first four years of Jack Welch's tenure and his efforts to change GE's
       strategy and planning activities and his efforts to make the firm more
       entrepreneurial.

Gold Star Co. Ltd. (9-385-264)

       -South Korean firms attempt to build position in the U.S. electronics
          sector as part of a global strategy is beset by antidumping penalties and
          Japanese competition. The volume strategy is explored.

Hyundai: Heavy Industries and the Shipbuilding Industry (9-385-212)

       -From 1974-84 shows how Hyundai captured share in a depressed
          industry.

Planning at Pepsi (A): Company and Industry Background (9-583-050) and Planning at
Pepsi (B): The Strategic and Marketing Planning Process (9-583-051)

       Formal strategic planning has been initiated two years ago. Describes the
          evolution and asks for evaluation.

L.L. Bean, Inc.: Corporate Strategy (9-581-159)

       -High growth mail order house needs to decide among growth operations
          and how to manage growth. A very popular case.

Moet-Hennessy Group (9-386-191)

       -Strategic and organizational problems of a French firm pursuing
          diversification.

Sears, Roebuck and Co. in the 1980s: Renewal and Diversification(A) (9-386-029)

       -The purchase of Dean Witter and Coldwell Banker and the
          implementations problems.   Videotape (9-997-001) is also available.

DuPont in Titanium Dioxide (B1) (9-386-069)

       -Examines the strategic logic and risks of preemption. Part of a series of
          six one or two page cases following E. F. DuPont & Co.; Titanium
          Dioxide (9-284-066).

Black & Decker Corp.: Household Products (A1) (9-587-057)

       -Acquisitions, the role of marketing in support of the brand transition from
          GE to Black & Decker.

Note on the Disk Drive Industry--1985 (9-586-040)

       -Historical overview of a dynamic industry and its structure with an
          emphasis upon the customers, channels and competitive trends that help
          to determine the key marketing requirements facing disk drive firms.

Griffin Corp (9-586-015) (TN 5-587-079)

       -Should the sales force of an acquired firm be integrated into the parent's
          sales and marketing organization and, if so, how.

Stafford Catalog Showrooms (9-586-017) (TN 5-587-051)

       -Chain of ten catalog showrooms is losing money and must decide whether
          to close some locations and how to regain profitable niche. Analysis of
          competition and operations within the industry is involved.

BankAmerica Corp.: Project Charles (9-385-246)

       -BankAmerica is considering acquiring Charles Schwab.

Orthoteks USA (A) (9384-057)

       -The implementation problems of a CEO of a U.S. subsidiary of a Swiss
          medical products firm. Has a series of five two-page follow-up cases
          detailing specific actions.

Novo Industry (9-389-148)
    -Worldwide insulin market in 1982
General Electric Co: Preparing for the 1990s (9-390-091)
    -Describes Jack Welch's tenure through 1980s
Honda Motor Co. and Honda of America (A) (9-390-111)
    -Describes Honda's unique style of management in its
     motorcycle business.
Images for the Masses: The Worldwide Photography Industry (9-390-163)
    -Good for industry analysis. Covers the industry in the
     1980s.
Olivetti Series A, B, and C (9-388-157) (9-388-158) (9-390-003)
    -Describes strategy up to 1987.
MRS Technology (9-390-158)
    -New hi-tech in an emergent technology
Original Italian Pasta Products Co.
    -Fresh pasta company takes on Number 1 in 1989.
U.S. Airline industry--1978-88 (9-390-025) (TN 5-390-169)
Atlas Copco (A) (9-588-004) (TN 5-589-076)
    -A Swedish firm attempts to gain distribution in the U.S.
     for its air compressor products--1986.
Babbage's: America's Software Headquarters (9-589-100)
    -Fast growing chain of retail stores--1989. How to manage
     growth.
Georgetown Leather Design (9-589-111)
    -Retail chain expansion plans.
Nissan Motor Co: Marketing Strategy for Europe (9-590-018)
    -Review of European strategy--1989.
The Procter & Gamble Company--(-592-016) 1991
    Dealing with environmental concern in Germany
Microsoft Works ((9-588-028) (TM 5-590-076)
    -Standardization vs. customization in global strategy.
Federated Industries (A) (9-585-104)
    -A declining industries case.
Colgate-Palmolive Company (9-593-064) (TN 5-593-064)
    -Position new toothbrush as mainstream or niche.
CF MotorFreight in 1992 (9-793-100) (TN 5-794-140)
    -Reach to deteriorating industry structure and competitive position.
Cray Research (9-390-066) (TN 5-385-316)
    -Discusses major changes 1985 to 1990.
Northern Telecom (A) (9-593-103)
    -The creation of a new telephone system for a small business market.
Mary Kay Cosmetics: Asian Market Entry
    -On entering Japanese and/or Chinese markets.
Intel Corp: Going Into OverDrive (9-593-051) (TN 5-394-020)
    -On managing a product line with rapid technological change.

Signode (A) (9-586-059) (TN 5-588-023)
Pepsi Cola United Kingdom (9-584 052)
Sealed Air (9-582-103)
HenKel (9-585-099) (TN 5-585-117)
SAS (9-487-041) (TN 5-489-078)
Microwave Oven Industry (9-579-187) (TN 5-585-125)
E.T. Phone Home
Federal Express (A) (9-577-042) (TN 5-577-189)
Pixley-Richards (9-482-063) (TN 5-584-069)
IBM: PS/2 (9-590-026)
Northern Telecom (A) (9-682-106)
Motorfabrikwerk S. A. (9-584-074) (TN 5-584-075)
Cray (9-390-066)
Note of the World Pharmaceutical Industry (9-583-168)
Ciba-Geigy Pharmaceuticals Division (9-584-018)
Concept Devices (9-582-052) (TN 5-583-134)
Computervision (A) (0-384-142) (TN 4-385-085)
Perkin Elmer: Data Systems Group (9-582-101) (TN 5-583-030)
U.S. Retail Coffee Market (B) (9-582-088) (TN 5-585-108)
U.S. Retail Coffee Market (C) (9-583-001)
Brim (B) (9-582-090)

Sources of Cases:

Harvard Business School Publishing Division
        Operations Department,
        Boston, Massachusetts 02163
        Tel 617-495-6117
Darden Educational Materials
        Graduate School of Business Administration
        University of Virginia
        PO Box 6550
        Charlottesville VA 22906-6550
        Tel 804-924-3009
Case Collection of the European Case Clearing House
        ECCH at Babson Ltd.
        Babson College
        Babson Park, Wellesley
        Massachusetts 02157-0901
        Tel 617-239-5884

INSTRUCTOR RESOURCES

Periodicals

Fast Company
Subscription Department
P.O. Box 52760
Boulder, CO 80323-2760
10 issues for $19.75
Subscriptions:(800) 688-1545
Education Program:(800) 553-9604
Web site: http://www.fastcompany.com

Comments: Relatively new magazine. The tag line tells it all: "How Smart Business Works." Articles in the current edition include: "The New Brains in Marketing" and "New Tricks to Track Your Competition."

Wired
P.O. Box 55690
Boulder, CO 80323-5690
12 issues $29.95
Subscriptions: (800) 769-4733
Web site: http://www.wired.com

Comments: Interesting magazine for new ideas. Offers contemporary and future views of businesses, especially the influence of high technology on businesses. One of the feature columns is entitled "Tomorrow Today" which is indicative of the content of this magazine. One of the important articles that appeared in 1997 was "The Long Boom," which discussed the next 25 years.

Fortune Magazine
P.O. Box 61490
Tampa, FL 33661-1490
Subscription: 26 issues $59.54
Education Department (800) 416-5138
Subscription: (800) 242-6162
Web site: http://www.fortune.com

Comments: Fortune Magazine has an excellent Education Program. They not only offer students a reduced rate subscription but they will fax to you an overview of the current issue with suggested ways to use their magazine in the classroom. See sample Fortune Fax Preview in the back of this section.

Journal of Business Strategy
Faulkner & Gray
11 Penn Plaza
New York, NY 10117-0373
One year subscription: $98 (+ $4.95 postage/handling). Published bi-monthly.
1 (800) 535-8403

Comments: A magazine for the Corporate Strategist. Offers interesting general strategy articles. The current issue offers "Reinventing Innovation" and a monthly marketing column.

The Futurist
Published monthly by The World Future Society
Web site: http://www.wfs.org/wfs
Subscriptions: (800) 989-8274
$35.00 annual dues

Comments: Great source of provocative insights into trends/forecasts. Publishes annual forecast that looks ten years out.

Other Resources

The Wall Street Journal Interactive
1 (800) 369-2834
Free with WSJ newspaper subscription

Comments: A great up-to-date resource for what is happening in business and marketing around the world. Allows you to print out articles on regular size paper. Very easy to use.

Harvard Business School
Teaching Materials Catalog
http://www.hbsp.harvard.edu
1 (800) 545-7685
Harvard Business School Publishing
Customer Service Department
60 Harvard Way
Boston, MA 02163
(617) 495-6117

Comments: Check this catalog out for new ideas in teaching materials. As an educator you can sign up for their on-line service to see what is new and also to download some of their materials.

Sloan Management Review
77 Massachusetts Ave., E60 100
Cambridge, MA 02139-4307
Yearly Subscription: $79.00
http://www.web.mit.edu/smr-online/

California Management Review
S549 Haas School of Business, #1900
University of California
Berkeley, CA 94720-1900
(510) 642-7159
e-mail: cmr@haas.berkeley.edu
http://www.haas.berkeley.edu – go to the
    news and publications list, and then go to
    the California Management Review
Annual Subscription: $50

Business Websites

American City Business Journal
http://www.amcity.com

Fortune Magazine
http://www.fortune.com

A.C. Nielsen Company
http://www.acnielsen.com

American Marketing Association
http://www.ama.org/homepage.html

J.D. Power and Associates
http://jdpower.com

American Demographics-Marketing Tools Magazine
http://www.demographics.com

Business Week
http://www.businessweek.com

CIO Magazine
http://www.cio.com/CIO

Forbes Magazine Online
http:///www.forbes.com

Red Herring Magazine
http://www.herring.com/mag/home.html
Access Business Online
http://clickit.com

Business Researcher's Interests
http://www.brint.com/interests.html

Forbes 200 Best Small Companies in America
http://www/forbes.com/200best

Hoover's Online
http://www.hoovers.com

Industry Net Online Marketplace
http://www.indsutry.net

Internet Business Bureau
http://www.ibb.com

NandO Times Business Section
http://www2.nando.net/nt/biz

Nijenrode Business Resources
http://www.nijenrode.nl/nbr

Strictly Business! Web
http://www.uni.com

Business Sources on the Internet
http://www.dis.strath.ac.uk/business

International Business Resources
http://www.ciber.bus.msu.edu/busres.htm

Totem Pole – Commercial Sites
http://www.totempole.com

International Business Resources
http://www.smartbiz.com/sbs/cats/ie.htm

Selected Harvard Business Review Articles

**Customer Intimacy and
Other Value Disciplines**
by Michael Treacy and Fred Wiersema
Reprint # 93107

Strategy as Stretch and Leverage
by Gary Hamel and C.K. Prahalad
Reprint # 93204

Strategic Intent
by Gary Hamel and C.K. Prahalad
Reprint # 89308

What the Hell is "Market-Oriented"?
by Benson P. Shapiro
Reprint # 88610

Strategy as Revolution
by Gary Hamel
Reprint # 96405

**Manage Marketing by the
Customer Equity Test**
by Robert C. Blattberg and John Deighton
Reprint # 96402

Sustainable Advantage
By Pankaj Ghemawat
Reprint # 86507

Making Strategy: Learning by Doing
By Clayton M. Christensen
Reprint # 97602

Brand Building Without Mass Media
By David A. Aaker
Reprint # 97107

The Fall and Rise of Strategic Planning
by Henry Mintzberg
Reprint # 94107

Realize Your Customers' Full Profit Potential
by Alan W.H. Grant and Leonard A Schlesinger
Reprint # 95503

Why Satisfied Customers Defect
by Thomas O. Jones and W. Earl Sasser, Jr.
Reprint # 95606

The Core Competence of the Corporation
by Gary Hamel and C.K. Prahalad
Reprint # 90311

What is Strategy?
by Michael E. Porter
Reprint # 96608

Strategy Under Uncertainty
by Hugh Courtney, Jane Kirkland, Patrick Viguerie
Reprint # 97603

What's Wrong with Strategy?
by Andrew Campbell and Marcus Alexander
Reprint # 97601

Discovering New Points of Differentiation
By Ian C. MacMillan and Rita Gunther McGrath
Reprint # 97408

**Should You Take Your Brand to Where the
Action Is?**
by David A. Aaker
Reprint # 97501

Contact: Harvard Business Review
60 Harvard Way
Boston, MA 02163
1-800-988-0886
1-617-495-6117

Recommended Books

Building Strong Brands
by David A. Aaker
Publisher: The Free Press, 1996

Competing for the Future
by Gary Hamel and C.K. Prahalad
Publisher: Harvard Business School, 1994

How to Drive Your Competition Crazy
by Guy Kawasaki
Publisher: Hyperion, 1995

Mass Customization
by Joseph Pine
Publisher: Free Press, 1993

Marketing Mistakes
by Robert F, Hartley
Publisher: Wiley and Sons, 1998

Relationship Marketing
by Regis McKenna
Publisher: Addison Wesley, 1991

The Discipline of Market Leaders
by Michael Treacy & Fred Wiersema
Publisher: Addison Wesley, 1995

The Marketing Revolution
by Kevin J. Clancy and Robert S. Shulman
Publisher: HarperBusiness, 1993

The Popcorn Report
by Faith Popcorn
Publisher: Doubleday, 1991

Top Management Strategy
by Benjamin B. Tregoe & John W. Zimmerman
Publisher: Simon & Schuster, 1980

Managing Brand Equity
by David A. Aaker
Publisher: The Free Press, 1991

Competitive Strategy
by Michael E. Porter
Publisher: Free Press, 1980

Creativity in Business
by Michael Ray and Rochelle Myers
Publisher: Doubleday, 1989

The Marketing Information Revolution
by Robert C. Blattberg, Rashi Glazer, and
John D.C. Little
Harvard Business School Publishing, 1994

Paradigms: The Business of Discovering the Future
by Joel Arthur Barker
Publisher: Harper Business, 1992

Clicking
by Faith Popcorn and Lys Marigold
Publisher: Harper Collins, 1996

The Marketing Imagination
by Theodore Levitt
Publisher: Free Press, 1986

The Mind of the Strategist
by Kenichi Ohmae
Publisher: McGraw Hill, 1982

The One to One Future
by Don Peppers and Martha Rogers, Ph.D.
Publisher: Currency Doubleday, 1993

Real Time
by Regis McKenna
Publisher: Harvard Business School Press, 1997

THINKING OUT OF THE BOX
THOUGHT-PROVOKING QUESTIONS FOR STUDENTS

1. Discuss how antitrust laws can backfire, penalizing consumers. Who is typically the largest group of antitrust naysayers? Do you think Microsoft's growth should be regulated? Should WorldCom merge with MCI? How do mergers affect individuals? The global economy? Is the merger boom here to stay or simply the result of current economic conditions? *("The Case Against Antitrust," pp. 40-44; "Microsoft: Is Your Company Its Next Meal?" pp. 92-102; "MCI WorldCom: Can It Rule Telecom?" pp. 118-128; "Mergers: Why This Boom Will Keep Making Noise," pp. 148-156)*

2. Evaluate the management style of AIG CEO Hank Greenberg. What are the pluses and minuses of Greenberg's control and, more importantly, his longevity as AIG chairman? Compare and contrast Greenberg's style of management with that of Jack Levy, managing director of Merrill Lynch's mergers and acquisitions department. *("AIG: Aggressive. Inscrutable. Greenberg," pp. 106-116; "Merrill Lynch Takes Over," pp. 138-144)*

COURSE CONNECTOR

	management	organizational behavior	finance/acctg.	economics	marketing	international	info tech	human resources
"The Case Against Antitrust," pp. 40-44	■			■				
"Who's Afraid of the Euro?" p. 52			■	■		■		
"Hasbro's Short-Toy Shortage," p. 72				■	■			
"Microsoft: Is Your Company Its Next Meal?" pp. 92-102	■	■	■	■	■		■	■
"AIG: Agressive. Inscrutable. Greenberg," pp. 106-116	■	■	■	■		■		■
"MCI Worldcom: It's the Biggest Merger Ever. Can It Rule Telecom?" pp. 118-128	■		■			■	■	
"Goodyear Wants to Be No. 1 Again," pp. 130-134	■		■		■	■		
"Merrill Lynch Takes Over," pp. 138-144	■	■	■			■		
"Mergers: Why This Historic Boom Will Keep Making Noise," pp. 148-156		■	■	■				
"The Day They Couldn't Fill the FORTUNE 500," pp. 159-160				■				
"Industry Wakes Up to the Year 2000 Menace," pp. 163-180		■	■	■			■	■
"On the Road," pp. 182-195	■			■				■
"A Downshift in Profit Growth," pp. 216-219			■	■				
"The 1998 FORTUNE 500," pp. F1-F70			■	■				
"Finally! A How Not to Manage Book," pp. 414-416	■							
"Confessions of an Online Moonlighter," pp. 443-444	■						■	■

FORTUNE PROFESSOR PICK

Carnegie Mellon management professor Robert E. Kelly has been a member of the FORTUNE Education Program since 1990. Kelley coined the term "gold-collar worker" in his 1995 book, **"The Gold-Collar Worker: Harnessing the Brainpower of the New Workforce."** His letter to the editor appears in this issue of FORTUNE Magazine. Congratulations, Professor Kelley.

APRIL 27, 1998

INSIDE THE APRIL 27, 1998 ISSUE

■ **"Microsoft: Is Your Company Its Next Meal?" pp. 92–102:** By marketing online products such as Carpoint, Home Advisor, Expedia, Microsoft Investor, and MSFDC, the high-tech company is extending its tentacles—and that worries competitors in the auto retail, newspaper, travel, and banking businesses. Some defend Microsoft's strategies by claiming the company is a scapegoat for businesses that fear any changes wrought by the Internet. Others point to Bill Gates's need to grow Microsoft, since most employees receive stock compensations. Gate's lieutenant, Pete Higgins, says the company's Interactive Media Group is simply trying to develop "products for a Web lifestyle."

■ **"AIG: Aggressive. Inscrutable. Greenberg." pp. 106–116:** Hank Greenberg provides a management case study in longevity: 31 years at the helm of insurance giant AIG. Even more impressive is Greenberg's legacy. During his tenure, he has increased market value from $300 million to $88 billion, while only once allowing earnings-per-share to drop. Not even the economic crisis in Asia, where AIG was founded, has stymied Greenberg. Last year AIG's growth rate was 15.9%! The one concern: AIG's fate after Greenberg's reign ends.

■ **"MCI WorldCom: It's the Biggest Merger Ever. Can It Rule Telecom?" pp. 118–128:** Just five years ago, WorldCom was a struggling cut-rate long-distance company with a college drop-out CEO. Today the telecom company is waiting for regulatory approval of its $37 billion merger with MCI—a deal that would give the new MCI WorldCom annual revenues of $28 billion and launch it from No. 210 to No. 33 on this year's FORTUNE 500. The merger would also better position WorldCom to be the largest carrier of Internet traffic—talk about a transformation!

■ **"Industry Wakes Up to the Year 2000 Menace," pp. 163–180:** The real difficulty in removing the Millennium Bug from software isn't cost (estimated between $300 billion and $600 billion), but implementation. Many large corporations are only 34% of the way toward making their computers "year 2000 compliant." There are many ingredients in this recipe for disaster: delays in addressing the programming snafu, the archaic nature of Cobol (the computer language used to write many of the problematic programs), a shortage of computer programmers, and an inflexible deadline.

■ **"The FORTUNE 500: A Downshift in Profit Growth," pp. 216–F70:** The FORTUNE 500 list remains the definitive scorecard of U.S. business, offering a variety of informative corporate measures. Aside from the airline and auto industries, corporate profit growth has generally fallen; total 1997 earnings for FORTUNE 500 companies grew by just 7.8%, compared to 23.3% in 1996. Rising labor costs, restructuring difficulties, inability to raise prices, and the Asian economic crisis help explain this decline in net income growth. Oddly, this trend occurred as 1997 stock prices rose by over 30%, compared to 21% in 1996. Mergers certainly helped boost stock prices, and even more dramatically, affected rankings of the FORTUNE 500. As usual, predictions for 1998 corporate profit growth are mixed, ensuring that only time will tell.

If there are problems with this transmission, CALL 800-416-5138.

Inside: General Motors Leads The Fortune 500

A PUBLICATION OF THE FORTUNE EDUCATION PROGRAM

PROST LECTURE NOTES

Chapter 1 – Business Strategy: The Concept and Trends in Its Management

Notes for discussion

[Show Slide 1-1]

Discuss the quotes from the front of the chapter and their implication in today's business environment. Allow students to bring forth their ideas as they relate to the quotes. Students frequently come up with more varied and insightful interpretations of the quotes.

[Show Slide 1-2]

"Plans are nothing, Planning is everything"
Dwight D. Eisenhower

[Show Slide 1-3]

"Where an absolute superiority is not attainable, you must produce a relative one at the decision point by making skillful use of what you have."
Karl von Clausewitz, On War, 1832

Use the PowerPoint slides as a method to introduce the concepts of this chapter.

Where appropriate, relate the information to current marketing issues.

Key Points

What is a Business Strategy?
[Show Slide 1-4]
[Show Slide 1-5]

Strategic Thrusts-The Search for SCAs
[Show Slide 1-6]

The Concept of a Strategic Business Unit
Give examples, i.e., Hewlett-Packard: Laser Printer Division; Medical Equipment Division; Electronic Testing Equipment. If possible, give examples from local companies.

[Show Slide 1-7]

The Historical Perspective of Strategic Marketing

If we understanding the development of Strategic Marketing as a discipline it helps explain and define where we are today and why. A good supplemental article for this discussion is "The Fall and Rise of Strategic Planning" by Henry Mintzberg (Harvard Business Review).

[Show Slide 1-8]

Chapter 2 – Strategic Market Management: An Overview

Notes for discussion

[Show Slide 2-1]

Discuss the quotes from the front of the chapter. This is a great opportunity to talk about windows of opportunity and the implications for the marketing managers who "keep their ears to the ground."

[Show Slide 2-2]
"Chance favors the prepared mind"
Louis Pasteur

[Show Slide 2-3]
"Far better an approximate answer to the right question, which is often vague, than an exact answer to the wrong question, which can always be made precise"
John Tukey, statistician

[Show Slide 2-4]
" If you don't know where you're going, you might end up somewhere else."
Casey Stengel

Use the PowerPoint slides as a method to introduce the concepts of this chapter. Where appropriate, relate the information to current marketing issues.

Key Points

[Show Slide 2-5]

External Analysis

Customer Analysis

Competitor Analysis
- Performance
- Image and Personality
- Objectives
- Current and Past Strategies
- Culture
- Cost Structure
- Strengths and Weaknesses

Market Analysis
- Size
- Growth Prospects

- Market Profitability
- Cost Structures
- Distribution Channels
- Market Trends
- Key Success Factors

Environmental Analysis

Internal Analysis
- Performance Analysis
  - Customer satisfaction/brand loyalty
  - Product/service quality
  - Brand/firm associations
  - Relative cost
  - New product activity
  - Manager/employee capability/performance

- Determinants of Strategic Options
  - Strategy review
  - Strategic problems
  - Organizational capabilities and constraints
  - Financial resources and constraints

Creating a Vision for the Business
[Show Slide 2-6]
- Core Values
- Core Purpose
- BHAGs

Strategy Identification and Selection
- Product-Market Investment Strategies
  - Product definition
  - Market definition
  - Vertical integration
  - Growth directions
  - Investment strategies

[Show Slide 2-7]

> In discussing the Product-Market Structured Growth Directions (figure 2.4) use examples to illustrate:
> (Market penetration) The wide-neck water/beer/drink bottles; Blue Diamond Ad Campaign ("We only ask you to eat one can of Blue Diamonds a Week"); hair shampoo instructions "Wash, rinse, Wash again."
> (Market expansion) Arm & Hammer Baking soda is a good example of how a company can pursue market expansion.

(A&H toothpaste; A & H deodorant; A & H laundry detergent, etc.)
(Product Expansion) Sony's continued expansion with new products (i.e., the mini-disc).
(Diversification) Sears getting into financial services business.

In discussing vertical integration the grocery store chains are good examples. Where before they bought bakery items they now have installed bakeries on the premises – an example of backward integration. On the other hand, if the bakery item supplier establishes a retail store to market their bakery items it is an example of forward integration.

- Functional Strategy Areas
- Basis of Sustainable Competitive Advantage

Selecting Among Strategic Alternatives
- Consider scenarios
- Pursue a sustainable competitive advantage
- Be consistent with organizational vision and objectives
- Be feasible
- Consider the relationship to other firm strategies
  - ➢ Balancing the sources and uses of cash flow
  - ➢ Enhancing flexibility
  - ➢ Exploiting synergy
- Implementation
- Strategy Review

Chapter 3 – External Analysis Overview and Customer Analysis

Notes for discussion

[Show Slide 3-1]

Discuss the quotes from the front of the chapter. The article "Why Satisfied Customers Defect" provides good supplemental material for use in discussing this chapter.

[Show Slide 3-2]
> "The purpose of an enterprise is to create and keep a customer"
> Theodore Levitt

[Show Slide 3-3]
> "Consumers are statistics. Customers are people."
> Stanley Marcus

Use the PowerPoint slides as a method to introduce the concepts of this chapter.

Discuss the changing demographics and current market research on the migration and changes of consumers.

Key Points

[Show Slide 3-4]

External Analysis
- Affecting Strategic Decisions
- Additional Analysis Objectives
- Strategic Uncertainties

[Show Slide 3-5]
- Analysis
- External Analysis as a Creative Exercise
- The Level of Analysis—Defining the Market

As an aide to this discussion, material from Faith Popcorn, John Naisbitt, or Alvin Toffler or articles from "The Futurist" can help bring to life the discussion on trends and future events. Students in the class will mostly likely have discussion points on this topic and it usually provides for a lively interactive session.

The Scope of Customer Analysis

Segmentation
- How Should Segments Be Defined?
  - ➢ Benefit segmentation

> Price sensitivity
> Loyalty

[Show Slide 3-6]
> Application segmentation

[Show Slide 3-7]
> Multiple segments versus focus strategy

Customer Motivations

[Show Slide 3-8]
- Qualitative Research
- Changing Customer Priorities

Unmet Needs
- Using Customers to Identify Unmet Needs
  > From unmet needs to new products
- Using Lead Users

A discussion on the development of the entire Post-It Note ™ product line is useful in demonstrating how a company can move from unmet needs to profitable product lines.

Chapter 4 – Competitor Analysis

Notes for discussion

[Show Slide 4-1]

Discuss the quotes from the front of the chapter.

[Show Slide 4-2]

"Induce your competitors not to invest in those products, markets and services where you expect to invest the most…that is the fundamental rule of strategy."

Bruce Henderson, founder BCG

[Show Slide 4-3]

"There is nothing more exhilarating than to be shot at without result."

Winston Churchill

Use the PowerPoint slides as a method to introduce the concepts of this chapter.

Key Points

Identifying Competitors—Customer-Based Approach
- Customer Choices
- Product-Use Associations

Identifying Competitors—Strategic Groups
[Show Slide 4-4]
- Using the Strategic Group Concept
- Projecting Strategic Groups

Potential Competitors
[Show Slide 4-5]
1. Market expansion
2. Product expansion
3. Backward integration
4. Forward integration
5. The export of assets or competencies
6. Retaliatory or defensive strategies

Competitor Analysis—Understanding Competitors
[Show Slide 4-6]
- Size, Growth, and Profitability
- Image and Positioning Strategy
- Competitor Objectives and Commitment
- Current and Past Strategies of Competitors

- Competitor Organization and Culture
- Cost Structure
- Exit Barriers
- Assessing Strengths and Weaknesses

Competitor Strengths and Weaknesses

[Show Slide 4-7]
[Show Slide 4-8]
[Show Slide 4-9]

- Obtaining Information on Competitors

Certainly with the widespread use of the Internet, competitor information is much easier to obtain. It might be useful for class discussion to discuss ways students how found that have been useful in their search for competitor information, i.e., competitor's vendor relations department, etc.

[Show Slide 4-10]
- The Value Chain

Chapter 5 – Market Analysis

Notes for discussion

[Show Slide 5-1]

Discuss the quotes from the front of the chapter.

[Show Slide 5-2]
> "As the economy, led by the automobile industry, rose to a new level in the twenties, a complex of new elements came into existence to transform the market: installment selling, the used-car trade-in, the closed body, and the annual model. (I would add improved roads if I were to take into account the environment of the automobile.)"
> Alfred P. Sloan, Jr., General Motors

[Show Slide 5-3]
> "Imagining the future may be more important than analyzing the past. I daresay companies today are not resource-bound, they are imagination bound.
> C.K. Prahalad, University of Michigan

Use the PowerPoint slides as a method to introduce the concepts of this chapter.

Key Points

[Show Slide 5-4]
Dimensions of a Market Analysis
- Size and Growth
- Profitability
- Cost Structure
- Distribution Systems
- Trends
- Key Success Factors

Actual and Potential Market Size
- Potential Markets–The User Gap
- Ghost Potential
- Small Can Be Beautiful

Market Growth
- Identifying Driving Forces
- Forecasting Growth
  - Demographic data
  - Sales of related equipment
- Detecting Maturity and Decline

[Show Slide 5-5]
> Price pressure caused by overcapacity and the lack of product differentiation
> Buyer sophistication and knowledge
> Substitute products or technologies
> Saturation
> No growth sources
> Customer disinterest
- Looking for Growth Submarkets

Market Profitability Analysis

[Show Slide 5-6]
- Current Competitors
- Potential Competitors
- Substitute Products
- Customer Power
- Supplier Power

Cost Structure

Distribution Systems

Market Trends

Key Success Factors–Bases of Competition

Risks in High-Growth Markets

[Show Slide 5-7]
- Competitive Overcrowding
- A Superior Competitive Entry
- Changing Key Success Factors
- Changing Technology
- Disappointing Market Growth
- Price Instability
- Resource Constraints
- Distribution Constraints

Chapter 6 – Environmental Analysis and Dealing with Strategic Uncertainty

Notes for discussion

[Show Slide 6-1]

Discuss the quotes from the front of the chapter.

[Show Slide 6-2]
"There is something in the wind."
William Shakespeare
The Comedy of Errors

[Show Slide 6-3]
"A poorly observed fact is more treacherous than a faulty train of reasoning."
Paul Valéry

Use the PowerPoint slides as a method to introduce the concepts of this chapter.

Key Points

[Show Slide 6-4]
Dimensions of Environmental Analysis
- Technology
  - Impact of new technologies
  - Forecasting new technologies
- Government
- Economics
- Culture
- Demographics

A good source of world-wide economic leading indicators appears in the back of "The Economist" magazine. In addition, The Wall Street Journal publishes U.S. Leading Economics Indicators each month with an analysis.

Forecasting Environmental Trends and Events
[Show Slide 6-5]
- Asking the Right Questions
- Trend Extrapolation
- Asking Experts
- Decomposing the Task
- Cross-Impact Analysis

Dealing with Strategic Uncertainty
[Show Slide 6-6]

Impact Analysis—Assessing the Impact of Strategic Uncertainties
- Impact of a Strategic Uncertainty
- Immediacy of Strategic Uncertainties
- Managing Strategic Uncertainties

Scenario Analysis
[Show Slide 6-7]
- Identify Scenarios
- Develop Scenario Strategies
- Estimate Scenario Probabilities
- Perform Regret Analysis

Chapter 7 – Internal Analysis

Notes for discussion

[Show Slide 7-1]

Discuss the quotes from the front of the chapter.

[Show Slide 7-2]
> "We have met the enemy and he is us."
>> Pogo

[Show Slide 7-3]
> "Self-conceit may lead to self-destruction."
>> Aesop, "The Frog and the Ox."

[Show Slide 7-4]
> "The fish is the last to know if it swims in water."
>> Chinese proverb

Use the PowerPoint slides as a method to introduce the concepts of this chapter.

Key Points

Shareholder Value Analysis
- Strategy as an Option

Financial Performance–Sales and Profitability
- Sales and Market Share
- Profitability
- What is Good Performance?
- Economic Value Added

Performance Measurement–Beyond Profitability
[Show Slide 7-5]
- Customer Satisfaction/Brand Loyalty
  - Guidelines for measuring satisfaction and loyalty
- Product and Service Quality
- Brand/Firm Associations
- Relative Cost

[Show Slide 7-6]
  - Sources of cost advantage
  - Average costing
- New Product Activity
- Manager/Employee Capability and Performance

Determinants of Strategic Options
[Show Slide 7 7]
- Past and Current Strategies
- Strategic Problems
- Organizational Capabilities/Constraints
- Financial Resources and Constraints
- Organizational Strengths and Weaknesses

[Show Slide 7-8]

From Analysis to Strategy

Business Portfolio Analysis
- The Market Attractiveness–Business Position Matrix

[Show Slide 7-9]
- Applying the Matrix

[Show Slide 7-10]
[Show Slide 7-11]
[Show Slide 7-12]
- Logical Alternative Strategies:
  - Invest to hold
  - Invest to penetrate
  - Invest to rebuild
  - Selective investment
  - Low investment
  - Divestiture

Chapter 8 – Obtaining a Sustainable Competitive Advantage

Notes for discussion

[Show Slide 8-1]

Discuss the quotes from the front of the chapter.

[Show Slide 8-2]
> "Vision is the art of seeing things invisible."
> Jonathan Swift

[Show Slide 8-3]
> "All men can see the tactics whereby I conquer, but what none can see is the strategy out of which great victory is evolved."
> Sun-Tzu, Chinese military strategist

[Show Slide 8-4]
> "Don't manage, lead."
> Jack Welch, GE

Use the PowerPoint slides as a method to introduce the concepts of this chapter.

Key Points

The Sustainable Competitive Advantage
[Show Slide 8-5]
- Basis of Competition—Assets and Competencies
- Where You Compete
- Whom You Compete Against
- Additional Characteristics of SCAs

[Show Slide 8-6]
- ➢ Substantial
- ➢ Sustainable
- ➢ Leveraged

An interesting discussion can evolve if you ask the students, "What companies have a sustainable competitive advantage today?" Microsoft, Sony, and Hewlett-Packard usually come up for discussion. It is interesting to have the students point out the SCAs and how the company achieved them. Also ask what companies HAD SCAs and lost them. Usually IBM and Apple Computer come up.

- What Business Managers Name as Their SCAs
- Strategic Thrusts—Routes to SCAs

[Show Slide 8-7]

> Low cost
> Differentiation
> Focus
> Preemptive move
> Synergy

The Role of Synergy
- Core Competencies

   Assign the article "The Core Competence of the Corporation" and have a class discussion on the attributes of core competencies.

- Capabilities-Based Competition

Strategic Vision versus Strategic Opportunism
- Strategic Vision

[Show Slide 8-8]

> A clear future strategy
> Buy-in throughout the organization
> Assets, competencies, and resources to implement
> Patience
- Strategic Stubbornness
- Implementation Barriers
- Faulty Assumptions of the Future
- A Paradigm Shift
- Why Are Organizations Stubborn?
- Strategic Opportunism
- Strategic Drift
- Vision plus Opportunism

[Show Slide 8-9]

A Dynamic Vision
- Strategic Intent

[Show Slide 8-10]

> Strategic vision
> Obsession with success
> Essence of winning
> Sizeable stretch for the organization
> Dynamic, forwarding-looking perspective
> Real innovation and willingness to do things differently

   Assign the article "Strategic Intent" and discuss examples of companies who exhibit strategic intent; i.e., Nike, Sony, Hewlett-Packard, Proctor and Gamble. You might also find it interesting to present some of the work from Joel Arthur Barker's "The

Business of Paradigms." There is also a video available for this material.

- Strategic Flexibility
- Strategy as Revolution

Assign the article "Strategy as Revolution" and discuss the concepts presented. The article "Sustainable Advantage" is another article that gives good insight into the sustainable competitive advantage.

Chapter 9 – Differentiation Strategies

Notes for discussion

[Show Slide 9-1]

Discuss the quotes from the front of the chapter.

[Show Slide 9-2]
> "Ever since Morton's put a little girl in a yellow slicker and declared, 'When it rains, it pours,' no advertising person worth his or her salt has had any excuse to think of a product as having parity with anything."
>> Malcolm MacDougal
>> Jordan Case McGrawth

[Show Slide 9-3]
> "If you don't have a competitive advantage, don't compete."
>> Jack Welch, GE

[Show Slide 9-4]
> "The secret of success is a constancy to purpose."
>> Benjamin Disraeli

Use the PowerPoint slides as a method to introduce the concepts of this chapter.

Key Points

[Show Slide 9-5]
Successful Differentiation Strategies
- A Successful Differentiation Strategy should:
  - Generate customer value
  - Provide perceived value
  - Be difficult to copy
- Two Approaches to Differentiation

The Quality Option
- Total Quality Management
- A Customer Focus
- Quality Function Deployment (QFD)
- Signals of High Quality
- Perceived Quality and Financial Performance
- Perceived Quality and Stock Return

[Show Slide 9-6]
Building Strong Brands
- What is Brand Equity?
  - Brand awareness

1. Organizational associations
2. Brand personality
3. Symbols
4. Emotional benefits
5. Self-expressive benefits
➤ Brand loyalty
➤ Perceived quality
➤ Brand associations

Chapter 10 – Obtaining an SCA —Low Cost, Focus, and the Preemptive Move

Notes for discussion

[Show Slide 10-1]

Discuss the quotes from the front of the chapter.

[Show Slide 10-2]
> "Never follow the crowd."
>> Bernard M. Baruch

[Show Slide 10-3]
> "The first man gets the oyster, the second the shell."
>> Andrew Carnegie

Use the PowerPoint slides as a method to introduce the concepts of this chapter.

Key Points

[Show Slide 10-4]
Low-Cost Strategies
- No-Frills Product/Service
- Product Design
- Production/Operations
  - Raw material cost advantage
  - Low-cost distribution
  - Labor cost advantages
  - Government subsidy
  - Location cost advantage
  - Production innovation and automation
  - Purchase of inexpensive capital equipment
  - Reduction of overhead
- Scale Economies
- The Experience Curve
  - Learning
  - Technological improvements in production/operations
  - Product redesign
- A Low-Cost Culture

[Show Slide 10-5]
Focus Strategies
- Focusing the Product Line
- Targeting a Segment

- Limited Geographic Area

[Show Slide 10-6]

The Preemptive Move
- Supply Systems
- Product Opportunities
- Production Systems
- Customer Opportunities
- Distribution and Service Systems
- Implementing the Preemptive Move
- Research on Market Pioneers
- Research on Early Market Leaders
  - Envisioning the mass market
  - Managerial persistence
  - Financial commitment
  - Relentless innovation
  - Asset leverage
- Follower Advantages

Chapter 11 – Growth Strategies: Penetration, Product-Market Expansion and Vertical Integration

Notes for discussion

[Show Slide 11-1]

Discuss the quotes from the front of the chapter.

[Show Slide 11-2]
> "Marketing should focus on market creation, not market sharing."
> Regis McKenna

[Show Slide 11-3]
> "Results are gained by exploiting opportunities, not by solving problems."
> Peter Drucker

Use the PowerPoint slides as a method to introduce the concepts of this chapter.

Key Points

[Show Slide 11-4]

Growth in Existing Product Markets
- Increasing Market Share
- Increasing Product Usage
- Increasing the Frequency of Use
  - Provide reminder communications
  - Position for regular use
  - Make the use easier
  - Provide incentives
  - Reduce undesirable consequences of frequent use
- Increasing the Quantity Used
  - Reminder communications
  - Incentives can be used
  - Efforts can be made to affect the usage level norms
  - The perceived undesirable consequences of heavy consumption might be addressed
- New Applications for Existing Product Users

Product Development for the Existing Market
- Product Feature Addition
- Developing New-Generation Products
- New Products for Existing Markets
- Product-Line Expansion:

- ➢ Will customers benefit from a systems capability or service convenience made possible by a broad product line?
- ➢ Do potential manufacturing, marketing, or distribution cost efficiencies exist from an expanded product line?
- ➢ Can assets or competencies be applied to a product-line expansion?
- Does a firm have the needed competencies and resources in R&D, manufacturing, and marketing to add the various products proposed?

Market Development Using Existing Products
- Expanding Geographically
- Expanding into New Market Segments
  - ➢ Usage
  - ➢ Distribution channel
  - ➢ Age
  - ➢ Attribute preference
- Evaluating Market Expansion Alternatives

Vertical Integration Strategies
- Benefit: Operating Economies
  - ➢ Steps in the production process can be combined, eliminated, or more closely coordinated.
  - ➢ Economies of scale are possible
  - ➢ The substantial transaction costs involved in creating a contract between two separate firms may be reduced
  - ➢ Economies related to information gathering are available
- Benefit: Access to Supply or Demand
  - ➢ Access to supply
  - ➢ Access to demand
  - ➢ Idiosyncratic products and services
  - ➢ Four types of specialization:
    1. Brand name
    2. Dedicated assets
    3. Technological
    4. Knowledge based
- Benefit: Control of the Product System
- Benefit: Entry into a Profitable Business Area
- Benefit: Enhanced Technological Innovation
- Cost: Operating Costs
- Cost: Management of a Different Business
- Cost: The Risk of Increased Commitment to a Business
- Cost: Reduced Flexibility
- Cost: Inward Focus
- Alternatives to Integration

- **Are Integrated Firms More Profitable?**

Chapter 12 – Diversification

Notes for discussion

[Show Slide 12-1]

Discuss the quotes from the front of the chapter.

[Show Slide 12-2]
> "Tis the part of a wiseman to keep himself today for tomorrow, and not venture all his eggs into one basket."
> Miguel de Cervantes

[Show Slide 12-3]
> "Put all your eggs in one basket and–WATCH THAT BASKET."
> Mark Twain

Use the PowerPoint slides as a method to introduce the concepts of this chapter.

Key Points

Related Diversification
- Exporting or Exchanging Assets or Competencies
- Brand Name

[Show Slide 12-4]
  - ➢ An image of high (or low) perceived quality
  - ➢ Attribute associations with the brand or product class that are helpful in the new context
  - ➢ Attribute associations that would be negative in the new context.
- Marketing Skills
- Capacity in Sales or Distribution
- Manufacturing Skills
- R&D Skills
- Achieving Economies of Scale
- Risks of Related Diversification
  - ➢ Similarities and potential synergy simply do not exist
  - ➢ Potential synergy may exist but is never realized because of implementation problems.
  - ➢ Possible violations of antitrust laws create an additional risk when an acquisition or merger is involved.
  - ➢ An acquisition is overvalued.

Unrelated Diversification
- Managing and Allocating Cash Flow
- Entering Business Areas with High ROI Prospects

- Obtaining a Bargain Price for a Business
- The Potential to Refocus a Firm
- Reducing Risk
  - Stockholder risk versus management risk
- Tax Implications
- Obtaining Liquid Assets
- Vertical Integration Motivations
- Defending Against a Takeover
- Providing Executive Interest
- Risks of Unrelated Diversification
- Performance of Diversified Firms

Entry Strategies
- Selecting the Right Entry Strategy

Chapter 13 – Strategies in Declining and Hostile Markets

Notes for discussion

[Show Slide 13-1]

Discuss the quotes from the front of the chapter.

[Show Slide 13-2]
> "Anyone can hold the helm when the sea is calm."
> Publilius Syrus

[Show Slide 13-3]
> "Where there is no wind, row."
> Portuguese proverb

Use the PowerPoint slides as a method to introduce the concepts of this chapter.

Key Points

[Show Slide 13-4]
Creating Growth in Declining Industries
- New Markets
- New Products
- New Applications
- Revitalized Marketing
- Government-Stimulated Growth
- Exploitation of Growth Submarkets

Be The Profitable Survivor

[Show Slide 13-5]

Milk or Harvest
- Conditions Favoring a Milking Strategy
- Implementation Problems
- When the Premises are Wrong
- The Hold Strategy

Divestment or Liquidation

[Show Slide 13-6]
Selecting the Right Strategy for the Declining Environment
- Market Prospects
- Competitive Intensity
- Performance/Strengths

- Interrelationships with Other Businesses
- Implementation Barriers

[Show Slide 13-7]

Hostile Markets
- A Hostile Industry—Six Phases
  1. Margin pressure
  2. Share shifts
  3. Product proliferation
  4. Self-defeating cost reduction
  5. Consolidation and shakeout
  6. Rescue

Strategies That Win in Hostile Markets
- Focus on Large Customers
- Differentiate on Reliability
- Cover Broad Spectrum of Price Points
- Turn Price into a Commodity
- Have an Effective Cost Structure

Chapter 14 – Global Strategies

Notes for discussion

[Show Slide 14-1]

Discuss the quotes from the front of the chapter.

[Show Slide 14-2]
> "Most managers are nearsighted. Even though today's competitive landscape often stretches to a global horizon, they see best what they know best: the customers geographically closest to home."
> Kenichi Ohmae

[Show Slide 14-3]
> "A powerful force drives the world toward a converging commonality, and that force is technology…The result is a new commercial reality—the emergence of global markets for standardized consumer products on a previously unimagined scale of magnitude."
> Theodore Levitt

[Show Slide 14-4]
> "My ventures are not in one bottom trusted, nor to one place."
> William Shakespeare
> The Merchant of Venice

Use the PowerPoint slides as a method to introduce the concepts of this chapter.

Key Points

[Show Slide 14-5]
Motivations Underlying Global Strategies
- Obtaining Scale Economies
- Desirable Global Brand Associations
- Access to Low-Cost Labor or Materials
- Access to National Investment Incentives
- Cross-Subsidization
- Dodge Trade Barriers
- Access to Strategically Important Markets

Standardization versus Customization
- The Customization Option
- The Costs of Creating a Global Brand
- Creating a Standardized Offering—The Lead Country
- Implementing Global Strategies Involving Standardization

76

- ➤ Centralizing decision making
- ➤ The international brand company
- ➤ Selective standardization
- ➤ Using communication and persuasion
- ➤ Team management

Strategic Alliances
- Forms of Strategic Alliances
- Motivations for Strategic Alliances
  - ➤ Generate scale economies
  - ➤ Gain access to strategic markets
  - ➤ Overcome trade barriers
- A Strategic Alliance can:
  - ➤ Fill out a product line to serve market niches
  - ➤ Gain access to a needed technology
  - ➤ Use excess capacity
  - ➤ Gain access to low-cost manufacturing capabilities
  - ➤ Access a name or customer relationship
  - ➤ Reduce the investment required
- The Key—Maintaining Strategic Value for Collaborators
- Making Strategic Alliances Work

Chapter 15 – Implementing the Strategy

Notes for discussion

[Show Slide 15-1]

Discuss the quotes from the front of the chapter.

[Show Slide 15-2]
> "The basic philosophy, spirit and drive of an organization have far more to do with its relative achievements than do technological or economic resources, organizational structure, innovation and timing."
> > Thomas Watson, Jr.
> > IBM

[Show Slide 15-3]
> "Structure follows strategy."
> > Alfred D. Chandler, Jr.

[Show Slide 15-4]
> "Never acquire a business you don't know how to run."
> > Robert Johnson
> > Johnson & Johnson

Use the PowerPoint slides as a method to introduce the concepts of this chapter.

Key Points

[Show Slide 15-5]

A Conceptual Framework

Structure
- Centralization versus Decentralization
- The Borderless Organization
- Alliance Networks
- The Virtual Corporation

Systems
- Accounting and Budgeting Systems
- Information Systems
- Measurement and Reward System

People
- Make, Buy, or Convert
- Motivation

[Show Slide 15-6]
Culture
- Shared Values
- Norms
- Symbols and Symbolic Action
  - ➢ The founder and original mission
  - ➢ Modern role models
  - ➢ Activities
  - ➢ Questions asked
  - ➢ Rituals

Obtaining Strategic Congruence
- Corporate Culture and Strategy
- Hit-Industry Topology

Organizing for Innovation
- Decentralization—Keeping Business Units Small
- Task Forces
- Skunk Works
- Kaizen
- Reengineering

Chapter 16 – Formal Planning Systems

Notes for discussion

[Show Slide 16-1]

Discuss the quotes from the front of the chapter.

[Show Slide 16-2]
> "Strategic Planning isn't strategic thinking. One is analysis and the other is synthesis."
>> Henry Mintzberg
>> McGill University

[Show Slide 16-3]
> "Those that implement the plans must make the plans."
>> Patrick Hagerty
>> Texas Instruments

Use the PowerPoint slides as a method to introduce the concepts of this chapter.

Key Points

The Formal Planning System
- Four Step Process:
  1. External/internal analysis
  2. Strategy development
  3. Strategy presentation
  4. The annual plan
- Planning Forms
- Advantages of a Formal Planning System
- Role of the Planning Staff
  - Planners as strategic programmers
  - Planners as strategy finders
  - Planners as analysts
  - Planners as catalysts

Review the article "The Fall and Rise of Strategic Planning" and use in the classroom for discussion. Students find this article very helpful in understanding the role of Strategic Marketing in a company.

- Top-Down versus Bottom-Up Systems

[Show Slide 16-4]

Pitfalls of a Formal Planning System
- The Spreadsheet-Driven Process
- Dominance of Short-run Financial Objectives
- Planning is Restricted to the Annual Cycle
- Plans without Soul
- Plans That Are Too Rigid and Detailed
- Lack of Commitment to the Final Plan

Modifying a Planning System—A Case Study
- Streamlining Reports
- Strategy Review Levels
- Flexible Scheduling
- Top-Down Strategizing
- Role of the Planning Staff
- Results

Getting Started

SECTION 8

CASE: NOTES ON THE BEER INDUSTRY

Given the following material and your own knowledge of the beer industry, address the following discussion questions. In doing so put yourself in the shoes of the top management of Miller and/or Coors and/or another firm.

1. Conduct a thorough analysis of the customers, competitors, market, and environment.

2. How does the market segment? What are the key customer motivations and unmet needs?

3. Identify the competitors of Miller beer. Does bottled water compete with Miller? How do the strategies, strengths, weaknesses, and characteristics of the major competitors differ? Was it wise to extend brand names like Miller, Bud, and Coors into the light category? The dry category? Into draft? What are the strategic groups?

4. Where are the major beverages in the product life cycle? What are the growth submarkets? What information would you obtain to generate a strategically useful projection of future sales trends of industry submarkets? What are the major industry trends?

5. What are the environmental threats and opportunities? How would you respond to them if you were Anheuser-Busch or Miller. Generate two or three viable future scenarios.

6. What are the strategic options as you see them for Miller? For Coors? Should Miller enter the sparkling water business? What additional information do you need to evaluate these options? How would you go about getting that information? What do you see as the key strategic questions facing the industry?

Selected Beer Market Statistics: <u>Beverage World</u>, March 1993, pp. 57-62; March 1994, pp. 65-70; March 1995, pp. 81-88; March 1996, pp. 34-48; April 1997, pp. 44-58.

	1992 Units	1992 Share	1993 Units	1993 Share	1994 Units	1994 Share	1995 Units	1995 Share	1996 Units	1996 Share
ANHEUSER-BUSCH	**86.8**	**46.2%**	**87.3**	**46.3%**	**88.2**	**46.8%**	**87.4**	**46.4%**	**91.1**	**48.2%**
Budweiser	45.4	24.1%	43.0	22.8%	41.4	22.0%	39.4	20.9%	38.6	20.4%
Bud Light	13.2	7.0%	15.0	8.0%	16.5	8.7%	18.2	9.7%	21.0	11.1%
Busch	9.9	5.3%	9.7	5.1%	9.2	4.9%	8.9	4.7%	8.8	4.7%
Natural Light	5.3	2.8%	6.7	3.6%	6.8	3.6%	6.8	3.6%	6.9	3.6%
Busch Light	2.9	1.5%	3.9	2.1%	4.0	2.1%	4.2	2.2%	4.5	2.4%
Michelob Light	2.2	1.2%	2.2	1.2%	2.1	1.1%	2.4	1.3%	2.6	1.4%
Michelob	2.7	1.4%	2.4	1.3%	2.3	1.2%	2.3	1.2%	2.2	1.2%
Bud Ice	NA	NA	NA	NA	2.5	1.3%	1.5	0.8%	1.6	0.8%
Bud Dry	2.3	1.2%	1.7	0.9%	0.9	0.5%	0.7	0.4%	0.5	0.3%
Bud Ice Light	NA	NA	NA	NA	0.2	0.1%	0.4	0.2%	0.4	0.2%
Others	2.9	1.5%	2.7	1.4%	2.3	1.2%	2.6	1.4%	4.0	2.1%
MILLER	**42.2**	**22.4%**	**42.7**	**22.6%**	**43.0**	**22.8%**	**42.8**	**22.7%**	**41.7**	**22.1%**
Miller Lite	18.5	9.8%	17.3	9.2%	15.7	8.3%	15.9	8.4%	16.1	8.5%
Miller Genuine Draft	6.9	3.7%	7.5	4.0%	6.9	3.7%	6.8	3.6%	6.4	3.4%
Miller High Life	4.8	2.6%	5.2	2.8%	5.0	2.7%	4.9	2.6%	5.2	2.7%
Milwaukee's Best	6.6	3.5%	5.8	3.1%	5.2	2.8%	4.6	2.4%	4.1	2.2%
Milwaukee's Best Light	1.0	0.5%	1.9	1.0%	1.8	1.0%	1.8	1.0%	1.7	0.9%
Icehouse	NA	NA	NA	NA	NA	NA	1.5	0.8%	1.6	0.8%
Red Dog	NA	NA	NA	NA	NA	NA	1.6	0.8%	1.0	0.5%
Miller Beer	NA	NA	NA	NA	NA	NA	NA	NA	1.0	0.5%
Genuine Draft Light	1.5	0.8%	1.8	1.0%	1.6	0.8%	1.3	0.7%	1.0	0.5%
Miller Lite Ice	NA	NA	NA	NA	1.5	0.8%	0.9	0.5%	0.5	0.3%
Milwaukee's Best Ice	NA	NA	NA	NA	NA	NA	0.2	0.1%	0.4	0.2%
Others	2.9	1.5%	3.2	1.7%	5.3	2.8%	3.3	1.8%	2.7	1.4%
COORS	**19.6**	**10.4%**	**19.9**	**10.6%**	**20.2**	**10.7%**	**20.1**	**10.7%**	**19.9**	**10.5%**
Coors Light	12.6	6.7%	12.7	6.7%	12.8	6.8%	13.2	7.0%	13.7	7.2%
Original Coors	2.9	1.5%	2.7	1.4%	2.4	1.3%	2.2	1.2%	2.1	1.1%
Keystone Light	1.8	1.0%	1.9	1.0%	1.8	1.0%	1.9	1.0%	1.9	1.0%
Zima	NA	NA	NA	NA	NA	NA	NA	NA	0.4	0.2%
Coors Extra Gold	0.6	0.3%	0.5	0.3%	0.3	0.2%	0.3	0.2%	0.3	0.2%
Others	3.5	1.9%	4.0	2.1%	4.7	2.5%	4.4	2.3%	1.5	0.8%
STROH*	**14.2**	**7.6%**	**13.0**	**6.9%**	**12.1**	**6.4%**	**11.0**	**5.8%**	**17.3**	**9.1%**
Old Milwaukee	5.0	2.7%	4.6	2.4%	4.2	2.2%	3.9	2.1%	4.0	2.1%
Schlitz Malt Liquor	NA	NA	1.9	1.0%	1.9	1.0%	1.9	1.0%	1.8	1.0%
Colt 45	NA	NA	NA	NA	NA	NA	NA	NA	1.8	1.0%
Old Style	2.4	1.3%	NA	NA	NA	NA	NA	NA	1.2	0.6%
Schlitz	NA	NA	1.2	0.6%	1.1	0.6%	1.1	0.6%	0.9	0.5%
Old Milwaukee Light	1.4	0.7%	1.2	0.6%	1.1	0.6%	1.0	0.5%	0.9	0.5%
Old Milwaukee NA	0.2	0.1%	0.3	0.2%	0.3	0.2%	0.4	0.2%	0.4	0.2%
Others	5.2	2.8%	3.8	2.0%	3.5	1.9%	2.7	1.4%	6.3	3.3%
TOTAL US MARKET	**188.0**	**100%**	**188.6**	**100%**	**188.6**	**100%**	**188.3**	**100%**	**189.1**	**100%**

	1992	1993	1994	1995	1996
ANNUAL GROWTH RATE	-0.3%	0.1%	0.3%	-1.2%	1.2%
PER CAPITA CONSUMPTION (gal)	23.0	22.6	22.5	22.0	22.0

* Stroh purchased Heileman in July 1996.

Howard Banks, "We'll Provide The Shillelaghs," <u>Forbes</u>, April 8, 1996, pp. 68-72.

Irish-type pubs are the rage all over the drinking world, and Guinness Plc. is prospering. In the past few years Guinness' sales have plateaued as Americans and Europeans have cut back on their booze intake. Five years ago spirits accounted for over 80% of Guiness Plc.'s operating profits. In 1995, the ratio was 75% and falling. Partly counterbalancing this loss, Guinness' share of the UK/Ireland beer market has more than doubled, to 5%. Worldwide, sales of Guiness Brewing, Guiness Plc.'s beer arm, have climbed by over 5% a year for the past few years. The key to this strong performance in beer is the growing popularity of ersatz Irish pubs all over the world. These pubs try to create an atmosphere of conviviality and warm welcome for strangers. They feature Irish food and drink and Irish music.

"Coors Targets The Growing Hispanic Market," <u>Marketing News,</u> February 17, 1997, p. 15.

Coors president Leo Kiely III announced that Coors is launching a campaign aimed at a growing Hispanic market as part of its plan to outperform the market. Company officials say between now and the year 2000, the Hispanic market is growing at three times the general market. Analysts say Coors is operating at a disadvantage because it's unable to control pricing and lacks efficiencies of other industry giants such as Anheuser-Busch.

"How Kirin Lost Its Sparkle," <u>Economist</u>, September 14, 1996, pp. 66-67.

In June, Asahi Super Dry edged out Kirin Lager as Japan's best-selling beer. When other brews are included, Kirin still has nearly 1/2 the Japanese beer market, compared with Asahi's 31.7%, but the company's 40-year dominance is increasingly threatened by its nimbler rival. The Japanese used to think of beer (and still often do) in the same way as they think of raw fish: the fresher the better. So Kirin built its breweries near big towns and concentrated on making good-quality lager. Liquor shops and restaurants, both normally mom-and-pop affairs, were easily persuaded to stock its products. This was vital: almost all the beer drunk in Japan was sold in such shops and, to a lesser extent, in restaurants. Big supermarkets and discount stores now sell 40% of beer drunk in Japan; as recently as seven years ago the figure was below 10%. Yet, while other brewers concentrated their marketing efforts on big shops, Kirin was loath to offend the small shops that had been its source of strength. The retailing revolution was partly responsible for another change that caught Kirin on the hop: shops increasingly sell cans rather than bottles. Cans are cheaper to stock because they take up less space. In 1985 only 17% of the beer sold in Japan was in cans; now the share is nearly half. Kirin was late both to invest in canning technology and to install vending machines from which to sell its tipple.

Even now, only a third of its lager is sold in cans and less than half of all its beer. Asahi has done the right thing where Kirin has done the wrong. It invested heavily in canning technology: more than half of Super Dry is produced in cans. It woos big shops: Asahi's products account for 40% of beer sales in large superstores. Its branding has been strong: it appeals to the young and fashionable. And its marketing is aggressive: Asahi's salesmen do the rounds of restaurants, for example, persuading them to stock its beer. If a big chain refuses, Asahi's president, Yuzo Seto, goes and badgers them himself. Brewing is a slow business, comparable to trench warfare. Yet there is still room for the fizzy to outwit the flat.

Gerry Khermouch, "Beer Marketing For Dummies," <u>Brandweek</u>, March 31, 1997, pp. 38-39.

As craft brewers gathered in Seattle for their annual conference last week, it had become clear that the business has changed markedly since last year's confab in Boston. No longer a forgiving arena in which gifted amateurs can thrive after learning by doing, the segment now is a tough, even brutal, business. Growth has slowed, business failures are on the rise, and it has gotten much harder to get beers out to consumers. Anheuser-Busch has counterattacked with ferocity as it pushes toward its ambition of controlling 60% of the market by 2005 and 40% of specialty beers.

Max Lenderman, "Gold Rush: In Northern California, A-B Takes On The Locals And No Prisoners?," <u>Beverage World,</u> January 31-February 28, 1997, pp. 1, 15.

Anheuser-Busch has decided to launch a barrage of new products tailored for the specialty, or craft, beer market. But rather than relying on its American Originals craft beer portfolio, or on other similarly positioned brews, the megabrewer is taking a different route to compete with the smaller players. If there is a mature and prospering craft beer market, Anheuser-Busch wants to be there as well with a locally positioned brand. When Steve Harrison, marketing and sales director for Sierra Nevada, drives to his Chico, CA-based brewery, he passes a large billboard urging Northern Californians to "Think globally, drink locally." He chuckles a bit at the irony: The "local" beer in question is not his Sierra Nevada Pale Ale, but Pacific Ridge Pale Ale, a specialty product brewed by the world's largest brewer Anheuser-Busch. The Golden State is the biggest, if not the only, territory staked out by A-B for this kind of micro targeting. The Mammoth Missourian has introduced ZiegenBock, a full-bodied amber lager available only in Texas and introduced to compete with popular local brew Shiner Bock made by Spoetzl Brewery. The company is also running Michelob Hefeweizen, a draught-only, Northwest-only wheat beer, which dovetails with A-B's equity deal with Seattle's Redhook.

Richard A. Melcher, "Why Zima Faded So Fast," <u>Business Week,</u> March 10, 1997, pp. 110-114.

With the beer industry going flat in the early 1990s, marketing executives at Adolph Coors Co. thought they finally had a product that would put some bubble into their business: Zima. Launched nationally in 1994 into the thick of the New Age beverage craze, Zima was defined almost entirely by what it was not: not a beer, not a wine cooler, and without even a color. A crowd of Generation Xers tried to find out what it was, propelling Zima to a stunning 1.2% share of the beer market almost overnight. But within a year, sales would fall by 1/2, from 1.3 million barrels to 650,000. Last year, they dropped an additional estimated 38%.

Bill McDowell, "In Craft Beer, It's 'Style' Over Brand Substance," <u>Advertising Age,</u> March 10, 1997, pp. 20, 43.

Craft beer brands are competing with thousands of other labels, representing a sea of small-name brewers, for the attention of an increasingly fickle consumer, trying to wrestle share in a beer market that grew less than 1% in 1996. Whether through subsidiary operations or line extensions, major brewers have become particularly aggressive recently in trying to gain market share in a segment first tapped by small, scrappy operations. Attracted by nearly a decade of 40% compounded annual growth and price points 2-3 times that of conventional beer, microbreweries and regional craft breweries continue to proliferate. But market demand shows signs of slowing. Industry experts agree that a shakeout is looming and say marketing and advertising will become increasingly vital for survival.

Jay Palmer, "Brewing Storm," <u>Barron's</u>, October 28, 1996, pp. 37-42.

Health conscious Baby Boomers have been drinking less beer over the past 5 years, and when they do drink, they are more likely to go for tasty "craft" beers, many of them brewed by small, publicly traded companies such as Boston Beer, Pete's Brewing, Nor'Wester Brewing and Canada's Big Rock. This change in imbibing behavior is roiling an industry --in this instance, the beer industry. Upstart brewers will supply 2.5% of the beer that is quaffed in America this year, and they are likely to supply 6% by the year 2000. In dollar terms, the new brewers' impact is actually far greater than those percentages suggest. The reason: craft beers sell for 2 to 3 times the price of ordinary suds. No doubt the higher price tag adds to the snob appeal. Traditional US brewers like Anheuser-Busch, Philip Morris' Miller division and Adolph Coors have been forced to seriously rethink their strategies. The big boys' latest battle plans could make life more difficult for the craft brewers. The large brewers are actively pushing their light brands and have entered the craft business themselves.

Greg W. Prince, "Planet Guinness," <u>Beverage World</u>, September 1994, pp. 41-47.

Bill Olson, president of Guinness Import, believes his company's recruitment process is gaining greater customer acceptance. Olson describes this new recruitment as a beer hierarchy, with consumers going from domestics right into micros or from domestics right through imports to the quality imports. Consumers now have an expanded beer repertoire based on mood and occasion. Olson dates a revolution in tastes back about a decade, with advent of brew pubs and New Age. Olson says consumers became more experimental and started looking for quality and fuller flavor. According to Olson, import drinkers aren't all necessarily clustered on the east and west coasts. "I think that's a myth that was closer to the truth seven or eight years ago," Olson calculates, "but in the last three or four years, you're seeing markets: Pittsburgh; Charlotte; Columbus; Houston; Phoenix; Miami-- markets such as that are just growing with high-quality premium beers including imports. We're very excited about what we call these emerging markets."

"Beer Scope," <u>Beverage World</u>, March 1996, p. 26.

You think of Molson, you think of Canada, you think of Canadian beers like the newest Molson label, Molson Red Jack. But is that all there is, my friend? No way, Jack. Presidente, from the Dominican Republic, is coming to the New York area via the Miller unit. The Big Apple is home to a majority of the Dominican emigrés in the US, and Presidente has 90 percent of the beer market in its homeland. Cerveceria Nacional Dominica, in turn, is distributing Miller Genuine Draft to the 10 percent of Dominicans who want something un-Presidente-ial. As for the rest of the Molson portfolio, senior brand manager Peter Reaske says 1995 was a good year across the board, particularly for the Foster's and Asahi lines. "The ice category," he notes, "will probably not meet volume expectations," but Molson Ice's share of the business is "going up."

"Buzz About Beer," <u>Beverage World</u>, February 15, 1997, pp. 43-46.

Industry experts discuss the future of the beer market in a rountable discussion:

GOLDMAN: It [the beer market] is growing this year [1996], about 1 percent. Each year for the last five or 10 years that we've gathered for this conversation we kept forecasting a 1-percent growth, and we were almost always disappointed. This year we got it. That's the good news. The bad news [for the big brewers] is that the growth is coming from imports and micros. A bit of good news for all brewers is that the mini baby boom generation is now coming of age, so the population of 21-year-olds and up-which had been flattening-will start increasing in the next year or so.

Anheuser has something that nobody else does: Bud Light. Roughly 20 million barrels strong, and it's having one of its strongest years in a long time. The two keys to Anheuser-Busch are this tremendous growth from Bud Light and the aim of keeping the decline of Budweiser at something other than malodorous. Budweiser has been dropping at around a 3-1/2-percent rate.

ROMM: Some beer trends include: First, consumers are willing to try new products. Second, consumers are willing to accept higher prices. And, third, we see significant gravitation away from low-end brands toward premium, superpremium and ultra-premium products, where much greater emphasis is laid upon brand building.

Anheuser sells 45 percent of US beer volume, but it controls over three-quarters of the industry's profit. So the question is: What's the health of the rest of the industry? It's very poor. The health of the producers of the other 55 percent of industry volume is very poor because they control only 25 percent of the profit pool. And Anheuser's share of profitability is rising, while the others' share is falling. Stroh and Heileman are partners now under a common umbrella, not so much because they so wanted to be together but because of the necessity of it. Coors will have to find a partner with which to consolidate to achieve long-term profitability. And although it's part of a very large and wealthy company, Miller's share of industry profits is declining even while its share of market has been relatively stable. Every major brewer but AnheuserBusch is in a very tenuous or an unhealthy state. And among craft beers, there are far too many craft marketers in the marketplace garnering far too little of the industry profit pool.

CONWAY: Which points to the scale issue. When you're Anheuser, you have a 45 share of industry volume, 75 share of industry profits. Miller has a 23 share of volume and maybe 17 or 18 share of profits. Coors has a 10 share of volume and 1 to 2 share of profits.

Stroh will clearly emerge as a stronger brewing organization with Heileman than without it, in part because the combined brewer can lower its cost of production and improve its logistics. They've already announced they will shut breweries in San Antonio and Baltimore. And only about 70 percent of Stroh's volume is branded volume; the rest is [low investment] contract volume. The question concerns the longer term: Stroh's marketing economies of scale remain an issue. And Stroh is strong in the malt liquor segment, with Champale, Colt 45, Schlitz, Bull and Mickey's. But this is an area Anheuser has said at times they will target, as the industry's last bastion of proportionate volume.

Constance L. Hays, In Search of the Six-Pack 2001, <u>The New York Times</u>, April 18, B1.

Among the top ten brands the notable changes in 1997 volume over 1996 were

Bud Light	10.6%
Miller High Life	6.8%
Busch Ligt	4.7%
Milwaukee's Best	-9.3%

The biggest changes in the top 25 were

Corona Extra	36.0%
Red Dog	13.6%
Pabst blue Ribbon	-13.3%
Icehouse	12.5%
Milwaukee's Best Light	11.1%

Based on 1966 data on who drinks beer

18-24 years	13.9%
25-34	27.8%
35-44	24%
45-54	15.1%
55 and up	19.2%

TEACHING NOTES:
THE BEER INDUSTRY

This should be used as a first case that will introduce students to methods and concepts of external analysis in an interesting and familiar context. During the external analysis discussion it will be useful to make a list of useful strategic uncertainties about the environment, industry, customers or competitors that will influence strategy. The case also allows a discussion of some critical strategic issues such as:

- The market scope decision--growth options. What is the logic of going into water, wine etc? Miller failed at the 7UP move because they could not crack the distribution channel which is tied up by Coke and Pepsi. What is the lesson there?
- The brand extension decision--what was the risk in bringing a name like Coors into the light beer area? Coors was hurt. Was that inevitable? Should the Coors name go on all the other categories the way the name Coke is? What are the risks?
- How to respond to industry pressures/threats. Many industries such as insurance, cable TV, and the oil industry face similar threats.
- The role of size as a critical success factor. How has Coors been able to pull it off?

I.   CUSTOMER ANALYSIS

A. Segmentation

Geographic--Is a regional strategy viable?

Age--Whether to market to the 18-21 age group, given MADD pressures, etc. Might note the power of sports associations to the 21- to 35- year old group. How much reliance should be made on event promotions?

Life Cycle.

Beer types (super premium, premium, import etc.)--How do they match up with life style?

Use occasion--How about a ____ with meals? On weekends? ("The weekends were made for Michelob" ads reduced Michelob consumption during the week.)

B. Motivations

Psychological, taste, thirst, alcohol, calories, social. How do current beers position themselves with respect to these motivations?

C. Unmet Needs

Great tasting low calorie beer (or has that been filled?)

Acceptable non-alcohol beer.

Beer for women--usually supports a lively discussion. How do you pull it off? Look at Virginia Slims. Coors Light did well but the Silver Bullet is not exactly a women's appeal.

II. COMPETITOR ANALYSIS

A. Identification

1. Should the market include carbonated fruit juice, wine coolers, soda pop, bottled water etc.? The answer will depend upon the scope of the strategy choice. Diversification issues will benefit from a wide scope.

2. What are the entry barriers for bottled water, soda, etc.? Why hasn't Anheuser-Busch done better at diversification?

B. Strategic Groups

National vs. Regional vs. Local.

C. Competitor Strengths, Weaknesses, and Problems

Anheuser-Busch

Dominant position in most categories.

Scale efficiencies in marketing & manufacturing.

Not diversified.

Miller

Big problem with Miller High Life.

Philip Morris backing with deep pockets and long arms.

Solid Number 2.

Weak record with new products perhaps until recently.

Coors

Quality reputation.

Fight with union is now over but image problem remains--
worth discussing.

On the move. Responsive.

Stroh

In trouble. Looking for niches.

Focus on popular price category with most of its brands.

Big brand Old Milwaukee is at a low price point.

Uses creativity and humor for Stroh.

Heileman

Grew via acquisition. Markets regional brands.

Strong in malt and non-alcoholic.

Is in financial trouble because of debt. Bond - the Australian firm that bought them - has crashed.

The Japanese--Asahi

III. MARKET ANALYSIS

A. <u>Size, Growth</u>

Since early 1980's, the beer market has been stagnant at best.

B. <u>Sub-Segments</u>

The product segments, size as % of total beer market, and trends are:

Light--growing.
Imports--Falling from 5% peak.
Premium--declining.
Popular--declining.
Super-premium--declining.
Malt-liquor--declining.
Low-alcohol category declining, but no-alcohol
  beer growing nicely although small.
Dry fading
Draft growing
Micros growing but very small

C. <u>Trends</u>

Event sponsorship.
Toward national brands/marketing.
Packaging changes.
Consolidation--The big two are picking up share from
  Heileman and Stroh.
Product proliferation big time--it is even more
  pronounced in Japan where there are gimmick beers
  (Beer Barrel, Beer Shuttle, Can Draft, Suntory
  Selection--Summer 1991) and taste innovations (Cool,
  Malt Dry, Fine Malt, Mild Lager).

D. Key Success Factors

Products that satisfy customers, tastes, and image.
Marketing.
Distribution.
Economies of scale.

IV. ENVIRONMENTAL ANALYSIS

A. Governmental/Legal

Consider proposals to increase taxes dramatically, to add disclaimers to all advertising, to restrict or eliminate advertising to sports events (particularly car racing). What impact will these initiatives have on the demand for beer? On marketing programs, particularly to colleges?

What impact will the container bills have (a deposit will be required on all containers)?

B. Demographic

What is the impact of an aging population on the demand for beer, which is traditionally considered to be a young adult's beverage? Move to wine? Or other beverages? Or new products?

C. Cultural

What is the impact of increased health consciousness in society? Has the trend toward "health beverages" such as natural juices/juice-based beverages (wine coolers) hurt the beer industry? What about the sentiment against beer advertising? And against the sponsorships of sports events?

D. Technological

What new beer types will emerge? What will be their impact and life cycle? What about dry beer? Malt beer? Other variations? In Japan, product innovation is driving the market. Will that happen in the U.S.?

E. <u>General Questions</u>

What are the threats?

Reduced demand due to legal, cultural, and demographic changes.

Competition of companies with other beverages.

What are the opportunities?

May further segment the market.

Eliminate weak competitors and take over their markets.

Improve operating efficiencies in the industry.

Meet new/changing needs of customers.

V. STRATEGIC UNCERTAINTIES:

A. What is the single most important environmental trend (legal, cultural, or demographic) affecting the beer industry? Is its effect cumulative? Is it the pressure for restrictions on advertising and promotions? Or product proliferation?

B. How will the "tastes" for alcoholic beverages evolve? What will be the future of the various product types?

C. Will the beer market remain stagnant? Will some sub-segments provide sustained growth? Which ones? Microbreweries? International?

D. Is it necessary to consider diversification into other beverages/food?

E. What strategies are competitors likely to follow?

VI. DISCUSSION QUESTIONS

A. Should Miller have come out with Miller Lite? Why did Coors Light hurt Coors? Was Miller Lite positioned too close to Miller (Miller time)? Was Bud Light a good idea?

B. Should Miller go into bottled water? Soda pop?

C. Corona was a very successful, almost fad, brand with no advertising. Why? It has cooled off some. Why?

D. What are the potential growth directions for industry participants?

- Market penetration--increase frequency, quantity, new uses for current users.

- Product expansion--new products for current users.
  New products--Microbrewies? Should Anheuser-Busch be more aggressive in the microbrewery area?

- Market expansion--new markets for beer.
  Geographic expansion--international?
  New segments--women?

- New product markets--diversification
  Related--new age beverages?
  Unrelated--other beverage/food products?

E. What should be done about the threats coming from those who attack alcoholic beverages?

- Work to distinguish beer from hard liquor and drugs.
  How?

- Continue to distinguish use from abuse particularly when driving--know when to say when.

- Mobilize the 50 million beer drinkers. How?

- Evaluate all programs and sponsorships with an eye toward this issue. How? What steps organizationally?

SECTION 10

CASE: XEROX: FROM THE FIFTIES TO THE EIGHTIES*

On September 23, 1981, Xerox Corporation announced that it was planning major cutbacks and a reduction in staff, a reorganization effort designed to make Xerox more competitive with the Japanese. C. Peter McColough, Xerox chairman, emphasized that "this isn't a crash program for 1981 or 1982. It's an attempt to restructure the entire business."[1] Six days later, McColough announced that he was stepping down as CEO, naming President David T. Kearns as his successor. Kearn's goals were clear: "If you really want to see how good you have to be to compete, the Japanese are the ones to look at. We want to be remembered as the company that took on the Japanese and were successful."[2]

While Kodak and IBM attacked Xerox's near-monopoly of the plain copier market in the mid-1970's, Xerox managed to hold onto its dominance in medium- and high-speed machines; as of 1981, it still controlled 60% of the market for machines over $40,000.[3] It was unprepared, however, for the arrival of the Japanese in the world copier market in 1975; moreover, it had not foreseen the need for lower-priced machines. As a result, Xerox's share of United States copier revenues declined dramatically, from 96% in 1970 to 46% in 1980. Stated David G. Jorgensen, an executive vice-president at Dataquest Inc., a market research company: "They have made colossal errors in being a fat, dumb, monopolist. And it's taking them years to overcome it."[4]

THE BEGINNING

Chester Carlson, the inventor of xerography, from the Greek for "dry writing," filed his first patent in 1937. He called his discovery electrophotography. He made his first successful image in 1938, then tried to market his idea to companies which included RCA, Remington Rand, General Electric, Kodak, and IBM. They all rejected his invention as unnecessary.

In 1944 Battelle Memorial Institute in Columbus, Ohio signed a royalty-sharing agreement with Carlson and began developing the electrophotography process. Their work caught the attention of Joe Wilson, president of Haloid Company, a manufacturer of photographic paper.[5] Haloid signed an agreement with Battelle in 1947 and began funding research. Wilson changed the name of the Haloid Company to Haloid-Xerox in 1958, eventually dropping Haloid altogether.

*Prepared by Rory Norton Bled and David Aaker as the basis for class discussion.

99

The Xerox 914 copier, thus named because it could make copies up to 9" by 14" in size, made its debut on September 16, 1959. It measured 42" by 46" by 45", weighed 648 pounds, and cost about $2,000 to build.[6] Fortune magazine later called it "the most successful product ever marketed in America."[7] It helped take Xerox from $31.7 million in sales in 1959 to over one billion dollars eight years later, to fourteen billion in 1985 with more than 100,000 employees worldwide. During its lifetime, between 1960 and the early 1970's, more than 200,000 914's were produced, for a total profit of over one billion dollars. There were still more than 6,000 in operation in the U.S. alone in 1985.[8]

The 914 truly revolutionized the copying industry. Where existing products used coated paper and were called coated paper copiers (CPC), the 914 was a plain paper copier (PPC). It also was easy to use and operated at the relatively high speed of seven copies per minute.[9] In the mid-1950's, 20 million copies were made per year in the United States on the existing equipment. A decade later, 9.5 billion per year were made.

In 1959, besides carbon paper, there were about thirty-five companies which made coated paper copying equipment, including Kodak and 3M. Copies cost between five and nine cents, but none of the other machines offered all the features of the 914. Kodak's Verifax machine, however, cost about $350, as did 3M's Thermofax. In order to be competitive, therefore, Xerox developed an innovative marketing strategy: rather than selling the machine outright, it leased the 914 for $95 per month, which included 2,000 free copies, with four cents for each additional copy. This pricing breakthrough, combined with the technical breakthrough, gave the 914 its phenomenal success.

Before introducing the 914, Wilson and Haloid were already making plans to distribute copiers internationally. In 1956 Haloid created a 50-50 partnership with The Rank Organization Limited of the United Kingdom. Rank Xerox had the right to sell worldwide, except in North America. In 1969 Xerox bought the majority one percent and acquired the Latin American operations.

Rank Xerox formed a 50-50 partnership with Fuji Photo Film of Japan in 1962. Fuji Xerox Company, Limited, is an independent company which handles copiers in Japan, Singapore, Hong Kong, Korea, the Philippines, and Taiwan. While Rank Xerox is an operating subsidiary of Xerox, Fuji Xerox revenues are not consolidated into Xerox Corporation's.

THE 1960'S

Haloid-Xerox's sales grew to $37 million in 1960 and to $59.5 million in 1961, with the 914 primarily responsible for the dramatic increase. On July 11, 1961, Xerox stock began trading on the New York Stock Exchange. Xerox defined its goals to its stockholders:

"But this is only the beginning. Our goal is to be a leader throughout the world in graphic communication, concerned primarily with copying, duplicating, recording, and displaying images. Today's machines work from visible characters. Tomorrow they may work, at great speed, from electronic impulses and invisible signals. So long as there is need for man to send information and either to copy directly or to convert the language of computers or other electronic devices into a form which other men can understand, there will be a need for making images. This is our field."[10]

Over the next seven years, Xerox brought out the model 813, a desk-top machine introduced in 1963 and marketed largely by Rank Xerox; the model 720, a faster version of the 914; and the model 660, a faster successor to the 813. It also introduced models 2400, 3600, and 7000, which had more features and were fast enough to make Xerox a direct competitor with offset manufacturers like A.B. Dick. Peter McColough considers the 2400, conceived in 1960 and introduced in 1965, to be the only really successful new product development effort between the 914 and the 10 Series, announced in September of 1982. Others either cost Xerox too much to develop in terms of money, time, and manpower or resulted in an inferior machine.[11]

In its early stages, Xerox had no formal product strategy. Technology drove the company. In the mid-60's, however, Wilson and McColough, who had joined Xerox in 1954, began to concentrate more on the structure of the Xerox line and the possible forms that competition would take. They focused primarily on the upper-end, high-volume portion of the market. As McColough says, "The Japanese, with coated paper machines, were pretty strong in the small copier business back in the sixties. So we didn't have a great interest in the low end because, while the volume of machines was substantial, the total revenue was not substantial compared to the middle and high end. More importantly, the margins were much worse than the other areas. It was not that attractive."[12]

Strategy Q, implemented in 1967, was the first formal strategy for Xerox. It divided the company's reprographics market into four segments: low-volume convenience copying, middle market, top markets, and duplicating. R & D was to focus on the middle and top markets with the goal of developing faster electrostatic copier/duplicators for corporate reproduction.[13]

While R & D was working on developing faster, more sophisticated products, marketing was to increase its share of the reprographics market with existing products. With this goal in mind, McColough, who became president of Xerox in 1966, concentrated on building the direct sales and service force. McColough felt that this force, in place from Haloid's photographic days, was crucial: "The 914 was incredibly more expensive and complex than anything else on the market at the time. The usual way of selling those copiers was through dealers. Dealers would not really be prepared to make the investment in parts that we required and certainly not be willing to make the investment in servicing that we required. We were convinced that the only way to proceed with that was a direct sales force."[14]

At the same time, Xerox began looking to diversify. In 1962, with revenues at $115 million, Xerox made its first acquisition: University Microfilm. Soon after, it bought a new-technology company, Electro-Optical Systems.[15]

At the end of the 1960's, Xerox had filed over 500 patents to protect its copying technology. While it never licensed its liquid toner transfer technology, the basis of its PPC machines, Xerox did license its coated paper copying (CPC) technologies at royalties of 2% of sales to many manufacturers. Perhaps because it had no immediate plans to use the CPC technologies commercially and, in fact, never did so, Xerox did not see licensing them as a potential threat to Xerox business. Yet these CPC technologies, which most manufacturers licensed from either Xerox or RCA, gave companies like Ricoh, Copyer and Mita the opportunity to penetrate the copier market and take market share from diazo copiers. When they eventually entered the plain paper copier market, they already had substantial experience in the industry.[16]

By 1969 Xerox had adopted an innovative leasing strategy for its customers, promoted by a strong direct sales force. It had already reached a billion dollars in sales, with 1969 assets reaching $1,555,197,000 and net income $161,370,000.[17] And there were no strong competitors in its market.

THE MAJOR COMPETITION

IBM

IBM introduced its first office copying machine, the Copier I, in 1970. It was a mid-volume machine which went directly up against the 914 and the 7000; it was Xerox's first competition. The Copier II was also aimed at this market. Although both machines were less sophisticated than Xerox's, they capitalized on the IBM name.

IBM's Copier III was announced in 1976. A machine which produced seventy-five copies per minute, it was not an initial success. It had a very long paper path which created frequent paper jams. IBM redesigned the machine and brought it out once more in November of 1978, replacing or retrofitting the original Copier III's.[18]

Because of this problem, however, IBM's reputation in the copying market was tarnished. The newest Copier III, the Series III Model 60, has been a successful machine, but IBM has never become the threat that Xerox had feared. It has avoided the low-volume market, continuing to produce medium- and high-volume machines which it sold through a large national accounts sales force and a geographic sales force. In 1985 it was fifth in worldwide revenues for copying machines.

Canon

Canon began developing technologies not protected by Xerox patents in 1962. It substituted cadmium sulfide for selenium in coating the copier's photosensitive drum and added another layer to the drum. It introduced its New Process 1100 in 1970, a machine which used dry toner and made ten copies a minute; it was positioned against the Xerox 720. It was sold in Japan, then introduced in overseas markets, excluding the United States and Canada, in 1972. Canon licensed the NP technology to Addressograph/Multigraph for an initial fee of $1 million, but A/M never marketed it.[19]

Canon brought out its second-generation NP machine in 1974. Called the L-7, it used liquid toner and was known as the "liquid dry system." The major Japanese companies were already licensing the NP technology; the Savin 750, in fact, used some of the Canon technology. Because its American licensees, A/M and Saxon, were experiencing financial difficulties, Canon decided to market the L-7 itself in the United States.

Canon might have been a success at that time had it let American firms market its L-7. Instead, their own marketing efforts met with disappointing results. Their decision to be the only Japanese company since the early 1970's to sell copiers everywhere under their own brand name cost them money in the beginning, but Canon became a household name; Ricoh, who originally upstaged the L-7 through Savin with the Savin 750, did not.[20]

The NP-80, brought out in 1978, was a big success because of its price and its aggressive advertising campaign. A liquid dry desktop model, it made 32 copies per minute. The NP-200, introduced in 1979, made Canon a leader among the Japanese copying firms. It was a twenty-copy-per-minute tabletop machine which had Canon's Toner Projection Development System, fiber-optics, and microprocessing. It also cost only $4000. Canon sold 30,000 in the United States its first year on the market.

The Personal Copier was another Canon innovation which cut into the Xerox market. The PC-10 sold for under $1000, the PC-20 for under $1300 when they were introduced in late 1982. Both came with a $65 disposable cartridge. The slower copying speed was unimportant for the target market which wanted a small, inexpensive, worry-free machine for the home or office.

Canon's goals have been to enter the mid-volume market through the 7000 Series, to develop color copying, and to capture the laser market. They also entered an agreement in 1984 to supply Kodak with mid-speed copiers.

In 1985 Canon was the world leader in low-end machines and the second overall company behind Xerox, with $2,178,000 in 1985 revenues.

Eastman Kodak

Kodak entered the mid-volume market in 1975 with its Ektaprint 100, a plain paper copier which soon became the industry standard for reliability in the mid-volume market. It was fast, making 70 copies per minute, it had a document handler that recycled originals, and it was the first copier to use a microprocessor, increasing both reliability and flexibility. Kodak has concentrated on the high end of the market with its two basic machines: the 70 cpm series, Ektaprint 100, 150, 200, and 225; and the 90 cpm Ektaprint 250, introduced in 1982, Xerox's only serious contender in the highest-volume segment. In 1985 Kodak also began marketing two mid-volume machines from Canon, another company known for its quality.

Kodak moved slowly into the copying business, taking time to develop products which would become the standard for reliability and to build strong service and marketing organizations. Kodak was still able to move into fourth place in copier sales in 1985. Mike Murray, vice-president in charge of copiers, explains why Kodak has been successful. "'First of all, technology,' Murray says. 'Second, staying power. We had the financial resources. Xerox and IBM knew that by price erosion we had as much staying power as they did. Third, there was window. We wanted the upper end, but we didn't realize Xerox was as far behind on technology as it was; that it would take them as long to respond as it did. Fourth, the industry, quite frankly, wanted a viable alternative to Xerox. Kodak had the reputation. We were quite welcomed . . . . The rest of it is all in execution. We had management skills. We had a solid service organization. We had a good marketing organization. We had a very strong manufacturing capability.'"[21]

Kodak was criticized for moving too slowly and missing opportunities to capture greater market share with its technology; the company felt, however, that it should proceed with caution because it was confronting two industry giants, IBM and Xerox. Furthermore, the high costs for entry into the copying business meant to Kodak that it could not afford any mistakes. So it continued at its relatively slow pace, meanwhile laying a strong foundation with its machines and its service.[22]

Xerox was lucky that Kodak took its time. Eric Steenburgh, product manager at Xerox, says, "'If IBM had had Kodak's product, we would really have been hurting.'"[23] Peter McColough is even franker: "'We were competing in a marketplace in that period with what we considered very inferior products. We were still using 3600's and 7000's. That was old hardware. It was reliable because we had worked the bugs out of it, but it wasn't what we wanted. If IBM with its superior marketing skills and their size had the Kodak machine it would have been a much different story. Frankly, I've never understood why Kodak was so slow in launching that machine around the world, not only in the United States.'" [24]

The Savin Corporation

The Savin Corporation was founded in 1959 in the United States by Max Low and his son Robert with the goal of developing the world's first plain paper copier. Five months later, however, Xerox would introduce its 914.

Savin was then forced to stay with machines which copied on zinc oxide, rather than plain paper, to circumvent the Xerox patents. In 1964 it introduced the Sahara 200, a machine whose rights Savin had purchased from the Minox Company in West Germany. Savin decided to concentrate its sales in the United States. It gave a license to market the Sahara 200 in Australia, South Africa, England, and West Germany to the Nashua Corporation of New Hampshire. Kalle Niederlassung der Hoechst A. G. of West Germany was also licensed in Europe. The A.B. Dick Company had a license to market Savin products in the United States.

Finally, Savin gave the Ricoh Corporation marketing rights in the Far East and Japan. Paul Charlap of Savin also set up an agreement with Ricoh whereby Ricoh would manufacture the machine which followed the Sahara and Savin would buy $3 million of its production. Savin ended up buying $10 million worth of the copying machines. Savin also gave up $5 million in royalties so that it could send a team of A.B. Dick engineers to Japan to help Ricoh, a company bordering on bankruptcy, improve its manufacturing. The manufacturing improvements and the marketing licenses boosted Savin's sales to $30 million by the end of the 1960's.

Savin meanwhile formed a team to find another way of getting around the Xerox patents. They were attracted to a liquid toner approach based on work done by an Australian named Ken Metcalfe. The team included the American firms Hunt Chemical, SRI International, and A.D. Little; plus Kalle, Nashua, and Ricoh. SRI and A.D. Little worked on commission; Hunt would get a contract for toner; Kalle and Nashua would receive marketing rights; Savin would receive royalties and sales; and Ricoh would manufacture the machine and sell it to the other companies. Their breakthrough became the Ricoh DT--1200 in Japan, which was introduced in the United States in 1975 as the Savin 750.

The Savin 750, introduced at $4,999, sold for far less than the Xerox 3100, forcing Xerox to cut its prices dramatically. It actually sold for less than Xerox's other machines' annual leasing prices. The Savin 750 averaged 17,000 copies between failures, where Xerox machines averaged only 6,000 to 10,000. It made twenty copies per minute, the first in less than five seconds. Xerox machines took nearly thirteen seconds. Savin sold through dealers instead of a direct sales force. The dealers contacted Xerox customers with an attractive alternative when their contracts expired.[25] By 1976, Ricoh had captured the top market share in units in Japan; by 1977, Savin placed more copiers in the United States than Xerox. Although the Savin partnership began encountering difficulties in the late 1970's, the damage to Xerox had begun.

In the early 1980's, Savin was continuing to market liquid toner copiers and was targeting the mid- to high-volume market with its new liquid toner process, the Landa Process, although it had been experiencing some difficulties with it. Benny Landa developed a Savin 8000 whose prototype produced better-quality copies than the 1075, but Savin dropped plans to manufacture the machine.[26] Savin had $448,000,000 in revenues in 1985, ranking ninth among the world's largest copier companies.[27]

Ricoh

Ricoh of America was established in 1963. It was not until 1981, however, when the agreement with Savin, Nashua, and Kalle was changed, that Ricoh was able to market its plain paper copiers under its own name outside the Far East. With A.B. Dick's expertise, Ricoh was able to upgrade its manufacturing operations in 1965, emphasizing a total quality control concept. Ricoh was awarded the Deming Prize for quality control in 1975, the first business machine manufacturer in Japan to receive this prestigious honor. In 1985 it had $1,926,000 in revenues, ranking third behind Canon and Xerox in sales of copying machines. Ricoh has maintained its reputation as a leader in quality control as well as in computerized manufacturing.

Minolta

Minolta did not enter the plain paper copier market until the late 1970's. When the Savin 750 came on the market at its low cost, it forced Minolta to shift to the PPC, as people were now demanding plain paper.

Although Minolta was late to market with a PPC, it did introduce several firsts: the first copier with fiber optics in 1978, the first copier with both enlargement and reduction in 1980, and the first automatic zoom lens in 1983.

Minolta originally sold through American partners, then gradually built up an independent sales network. Like Ricoh, Minolta has earned a good reputation for its automated plants and its technology.[28] In 1985 it had $743,000,000 in revenues, ranking seventh in the world. among copier firms.

THE 1970'S

The 1970's began with a warning to Xerox: On April 22, 1970, IBM introduced its first office copying machine, the Copier I. It could only produce ten copies per minute, could not use cut-sheet paper, and could not copy from books, but it was made by IBM, a top American company. It didn't matter that the Xerox 7000 could run sixty copies per minute, make reductions, and copy on both sides of the paper; Xerox customers still cancelled orders and signed on with IBM.[29]

Legal Battles

Xerox retaliated immediately by suing IBM for infringement on twenty-two patents and misuse of trade secret information. These suits established a pattern of legal confrontation which would last throughout the decade.

In 1972, the FTC accused Xerox of illegally monopolizing the office copier business. This was a landmark monopoly case, as the FTC was entering into an area normally reserved for the Justice Department. It was also seeking to make Xerox divest itself of its foreign partners, Rank Xerox and Fuji Xerox, something no American company had ever been forced to do.[30]

SCM, an office equipment manufacturer, began another lawsuit in 1973, suing Xerox for antitrust violations. The Van Dyk Research Corporation followed suit in 1975. Then IBM countersued Xerox.

The FTC case was settled in 1975; Xerox agreed in late 1974 to make 1700 of its patents available to competitors. It was allowed, however, to keep Rank Xerox and Fuji Xerox. The FTC had been concerned not only because of Xerox's wealth of patents, but also because Xerox was patenting developments it never intended to pursue commercially, thus erecting one more entry barrier for its potential competitors. James Halverson, director of the FTC's Bureau of Competition, was to the point: "'I will be dissatisfied if Xerox's market share isn't significantly diminished in several years.'"[31] In 1974, this market share amounted to 85 percent of the plain paper copier business worldwide. Halverson would not be disappointed: Xerox's profits declined in 1975, for the first time since 1951, and the company lost market share. The consent decree also banned the favorable pricing schedules Xerox gave to customers leasing several machines; this strategy had created another entry barrier for competitors.

All these lawsuits took time, money, and managerial attention away from Xerox's business itself. One reason that Xerox settled with the FTC was just to concentrate on its private lawsuits. Xerox spent $23.3 million on the SCM case alone from 1975 to 1978, not including the time and expenses of Xerox executives who were diverted by lawsuits. McColough himself averaged thirty to forty days away from his position as CEO because of the SCM case.[32] In the end, the jury awarded SCM $11.3 million in damages, an award set aside by U.S. District Judge Jon Newman, who said that patent laws forbade financial liability for companies protecting their inventions. It was decided, however, and upheld by the U.S. Supreme Court, that Xerox had enjoyed an 'absolute monopoly' in plain paper copiers from 1960 to 1970.[33]

The Van Dyk company lost its trial, and Xerox and IBM finally settled their disputes by agreeing to share their copier know-how for the five years, from 1978 to 1983. IBM also agreed to pay Xerox $25 million.

Products

Xerox had long prided itself on its superior technology. Yet, as Mike Murray, Kodak's vice-president in charge of copiers, observed, Xerox actually lagged behind in product development. In the 1970's, it only introduced three completely new machines: the 4000, the 3100, and the 9200. The 3100 was initially a success when introduced in 1973, although it would prove incapable of competing against the Savin 750 in 1975 in terms of both price and quality. The 4000 was not a success. As Shelby Carter, head of the U.S. sales division from 1975 to 1981, puts it: "We had nothing but refried beans in the marketplace."[34] The 9200, introduced in 1974, while a successful machine both financially and in terms of reliability, took eight years and more than $300 million to develop. For Xerox to have grown during this decade as it did was more a tribute to the sales force than to product quality.

The Office-of-the-Future

A major strategic thrust for Xerox in the 1970's was the Office-of-the-Future, in which the copier was only one instrument of communication. Xerox purchased the computer firm, Scientific Data Systems of El Segundo, California for almost $ 1 billion in stock in 1969, and changed its name to Xerox Data Systems. The goal in acquiring this computer company was to enter the computer business without having to start from the ground up and to build for people what McColough called "'structures of information which they will find flexible, functional, and effective."[35]

To that end, Xerox poured money into XDS. Despite these expenditures, XDS began losing money in 1970. Industry sales had slumped and XDS, short on R & D expertise, could not develop the products Xerox needed to enter the business data processing market. The Rochester technology group stopped doing research on mainframe hardware and concentrated on peripheral development. By 1972 XDS had lost $100 million before taxes.[36] In 1975, after six years of losses, including $84 million in the second quarter of 1975, Xerox arranged with Honeywell to maintain and service the base it had already installed. It then closed down XDS.

While the decision to close XDS may have resulted from the large losses, XDS was actually doing well in 1975, with growing orders and enthusiasm about the XDS 550 and 560 from its customers. Nonetheless, it would have taken an estimated $150 to $200 million in further investments for XDS to break even by 1980, and Xerox was not willing to make the commitment. As Peter McColough said, "The computer mainframe was not at the heart of what we wanted to do. If it were, we would have had to stomach our losses..."[37]

Xerox purchased several computer peripheral companies in the 1970's: Diablo Systems, Versatec, and Shugart Associates. Although they were computer-related businesses and Xerox was looking to enter the computerized office industry, it did not pay enough attention to its new subsidiaries. Shugart's disk drive business ended up being closed in 1981.[38] The Diablo "Daisy Wheel" was eventually incorporated into a typewriter module for a word processor faster than IBM's "golf ball." This Memorywriter, developed with a lot of market research and attention to customer needs, has been a big success for Xerox. One reason is its quality; the other was the fact that it is marketed by the Xerox copier sales force rather than the Office Product's Division's own sales force.[39]

One of the problems Xerox encountered in its organization was trying to coordinate business units located in Rochester, El Segundo, Palo Alto, and Dallas. It had also moved its corporate offices from Rochester to Stamford, Connecticut. There were two business lines, copiers and computers, with too many layers of bureaucracy and too many miles separating them. There were so many functional units that planning and implementation became paralyzed. Product planning, engineering, and manufacturing did not even meet until they reached Stamford.

Market Segments

In the copying machine industry, there are essentially four segments: low-volume, mid-volume, high-volume, and supplies.

Low-Volume

Low-volume copying machines, capable of producing up to 5,000 copies per month, retailed for less than $4,000 in the mid-1980's. This was the area dominated by the Japanese. In fact, Xerox's only really successful entry has been via its Japanese partner, Fuji Xerox. Xerox did bring out the 3100 in 1973, but in 1975 it was selling for $12,000. When Savin and Ricoh brought out their 750 in July 1975 for $4,995, Xerox cut prices on the 3100 to $4,400. The 3100, however, was too poorly designed to be competitive, even at the new price.

Fuji Xerox had offered to export its 2200, introduced in Japan in 1973, to the United States, but Xerox refused the offer. Toshio Arima, now manager of corporate planning at Fuji Xerox, tried to convince Rochester to accept the 2200. "'We laid it out in front of them,' he said. 'We said a Konishiroku machine is coming, a Ricoh machine is coming. But they didn't believe it. For some internal reasons we didn't understand, they said 'no' to us.'"[40] Xerox did not take a Fuji Xerox machine (the 2300) until 1979, although Fuji had been shipping to the rest of the Xerox territories since 1977.[41] Had Xerox acted earlier, it undoubtedly would not have lost so much market share to the Japanese, and Fuji Xerox's position in Japan would have been strengthened.

Because many low-end machines are also personal copiers which are used in small businesses or in the home, the customer needs something requiring little service.

109

Parts like the cartridge are disposable and easily replaced by the customer. These machines are usually sold through distribution channels different from Xerox's traditional direct sales force: mass market retailers, direct mail firms, and office equipment or computer dealers. This is the segment where Canon was the leader in the mid-1980's.[42]

Mid-Volume

In the mid-1980's, mid-volume machines cost up to $60,000 and were capable of producing up to 100,000 copies per month. The Japanese, like Ricoh and Canon, were putting price pressure on Xerox at the low end of this segment, where machines sold for about $10,000. At the top end were IBM and Kodak, although the IBM Series III/Model 60 was not as sophisticated as the Xerox 1075 and the Ektaprint 225.

Kodak, then, was Xerox's main competitor at the top end of this arena. And Kodak, like Xerox, wanted to avoid the price-cutting techniques of the Japanese.

Service is much more important in this segment than in the low-volume. Kodak had the best reputation for service, with Xerox close behind, and the Japanese trailing.[43]

High-Volume

The high-volume segment was the area where Xerox had the least competition in the mid-1980's. Neither IBM nor the Japanese seemed interested in this market; Xerox's only competition came from the Kodak Ektaprint 250. Xerox had over 75 percent of world market share, and its 9000 series had proven highly profitable, accounting for more than $1 billion in annual sales. The 9000 was first introduced in 1974, competing with offset printing because of its productivity advantages. It could not, however, compete on long runs because offset is a cheaper process. Xerox responded to this cost dilemma by using the sales strategy of Dave Myerscough, marketing executive at Xerox: it leased fully-depreciated 9000's at $1800, a price which included all the copies a customer could make.[44]

Supplies

Copiers are used in conjunction with supplies like paper and toner. Most plain-paper copiers use dry toner now, although some of the Japanese machines use liquid toner.

Xerox was the industry's low-cost producer of xerographic supplies in the mid-1980's. Paper was responsible for about $500 million in annual revenue for Xerox and $25 million in profit.

Problems

One of Xerox's major problems in the 1970's was its focus on making the largest, fastest, and fanciest machines. It paid far less attention to reliability, and was therefore not prepared to compete with machines like the Kodak Ektaprint. It also ignored cost factors, not conscientiously sourcing its materials for low-cost inputs; it further compounded the problem by overloading its organization with personnel. When machines like the Savin 750 were introduced, Xerox could not compete, in terms of both price and quality.

Despite its fat, layered bureaucracy, Xerox did not see far enough to deploy its marketing staff in the field of customer and marketing research. Such a stance was perhaps understandable in the 1960's when Xerox had no competition and felt confident that its patents would protect it against entrants into the PPC market. This ultimately proved shortsighted, however. Xerox gave no thought to the fact that its customers might be willing to trade speed for price and reliability or that they might prefer to have more, smaller, and slower machines rather than a few large, faster ones.

Finally, the decision-making process at Xerox, as it had developed over the years, was so slow and unwieldy that Xerox could not have recouped in time to prevent the incursion by Kodak and the Japanese into its markets. Not only were there problems of geographic coordination among Rochester, Stamford, Palo Alto, and Dallas; the process of getting a product from design to implementation was painfully complex. In the first place, product planning, engineering, and manufacturing didn't converge until decision-making was at the executive level in Stamford. Second, each of these three organizations had its own functional units and hierarchy, lengthening the process of the decisions. A product would first go to drafting, then to detailing and to service engineering. If the drawing were approved, it would be passed on to the manufacturing engineering organization. Throughout, it would be subjected to a system adopted from NASA of staged program management, which entailed constant review and critiquing of products.

Furthermore, the total Xerox system was built around matrix management where, as Jim Kearney, an engineer and manager at Xerox says, "'No one takes the blame for anything. Everyone opens their kimono for everyone else to see. Everyone shares. No one really cares about actually completing projects. In fact, people think it's their job to not complete projects. You're promoted for not taking risks because the company never is exposed.'"[45]

Many of the controls instituted during this period were the result of Archie McCardell, brought to Xerox from Ford by McColough to be executive vice-president in charge of operations in 1966. At the time, Xerox was growing so quickly that it had few systems or controls. McCardell helped implement Strategy Q and the matrix system. He also worked with McColough and the Flavin Committee, chaired by Joe Flavin, a Xerox executive vice-president and former IBM executive. The Flavin report came out in 1972, and shortly thereafter Xerox reorganized into three groups: 1) the Information Systems Group for marketing; 2) the Information Technology Group for engineering and manufacturing; and 3) the Business Development Group for product planning, market research, and overall business planning.[46] While these divisions were to address the concern with the "Architecture of Information," they did little to aide communication and decision making within Xerox. It wasn't until the McKinsey Study commissioned by Xerox came out in 1977 that real attacks against engineering blindness and the Xerox bureaucracy were made. McCardell, now Xerox president, left, and Dave Kearns replaced him.[47]

McCardell also ignored the Japanese threat, perhaps an influence left from his days at Ford, where the automaker showed little concern for smaller Japanese cars. Analyst James Abegglen told President McCardell in 1970, along with other Xerox executives, that "Japan was the world's biggest market for copiers. If you put out a small machine that pumped out copies slowly but effectively, there was going to be one helluva market. That was Xerox's soft underbelly; to come up underneath that animal, the Xerox 914, on price with a smaller machine." McCardell's purported answer was, "So what?"[48]

With the McKinsey Study, Xerox began once more to reorganize and to address the threat of competition. It could not move fast enough, however; between 1976 and 1982, Xerox's share of worldwide copier revenues had dropped from 82 to 41 percent. It wasn't until the introduction of the 10 Series of copiers in 1982 that Xerox was able to stop the decline.[49]

QUESTIONS FOR DISCUSSION

1. Identify and evaluate Xerox strategy in the 1960's.

2. What entry barriers did Xerox create in the 1960's?

3. Identify and evaluate the strategy of IBM, Kodak, Ricoh/Savin, Canon, and Minolta. How did each overcome Xerox's entry barriers?

4. Why did Xerox lose position in the 1970's?

5. What were the strengths and weaknesses of Xerox in 1980?

6. What should Xerox do to come back in the 1980's?

FOOTNOTES

[1]Business Week, October 12, 1981, p. 126.

[2]Ibid., p. 126.

[3]Ibid., p. 127.

[4]Ibid., p. 126.

[5]John Hillkirk and Gary Jacobson, Xerox: American Samurai, Macmillan, 1986, pp. 55-57.

[6]Ibid., p. 64.

[7]Ibid., p. 56.

[8]Ibid., p. 60.

[9]Ibid., p. 61.

[10]James Brian Quinn, Xerox Corporation (A), The Amos Tuck School of Business Administration, Dartmouth College, Hanover, New Hampshire, 1977, p. 9.

[11]Op. cit., Hillkirk and Jacobson, p. 80.

[12]Ibid., p. 205.

[13]James Brian Quinn, Xerox Corporation (B), The Amos Tuck School of Business Administration, Dartmouth College, Hanover, New Hampshire, 1977, p. 4.

[14]Op. cit., Hillkirk and Jacobson, p. 209.

[15]Ibid., p. 68.

[16]Yoko Ishikura, under the supervision of Professor Michael E. Porter, Harvard Business School, Boston, Massachusetts, 1983, p. 15.

[17]Op. cit., Amos Tuck (A), Exhibits XII and XIII.

[18]Op. cit., Hillkirk and Jacobson, p. 79.

[19]Ibid., p. 143.

[20]Ibid., p. 144.

[21]Ibid., p. 89.

[22]Ibid., pp. 87-89.

[23]Ibid., p. 80.

[24]Ibid., p. 80.

[25]Ibid., pp. 131-134.

[26]Ibid., p. 161.

[27]Ibid., p. 14.

[28]Ibid., pp. 137-138.

[29]Ibid., p. 69.

[30]Ibid., p. 71.

[31]Ibid., p. 72.

[32]Ibid., p. 73.

[33]Ibid., p. 73.

[34]Ibid., p. 70.

[35]Op. cit., Amos Tuck (B), p. 6.

[36]9Ibid., p. 7.

[37]Ibid., p. 13.

[38]Op. cit., Hillkirk and Jacobson, p. 78.

[39]Ibid., p. 267.

[40]Ibid., p. 303.

[41]Ibid., pp. 298-304.

[42]Ibid., p. 20.

[43]Ibid., pp. 21-22.

[44]Ibid., p. 290.

[45]Ibid., p. 186.

[46]Op. cit., Amos Tuck (B), p. 8.

[47]Op. cit., Hillkirk and Jacobson, p. 179.

[48]Ibid., p. 124.

---

[49]Ibid., p. 3.

TEACHING NOTES:
XEROX: FROM THE FIFTIES TO THE EIGHTIES

The case describes Xerox and the copier industry through the mid-eighties. It can rather easily occupy two days, with the first day on the sixties and the second on the seventies and the eighties. The objectives are to:

1. Identify the key elements of a business strategy (Xerox and its competitors) and discuss their implications for the future competitive position.
2. Identify barriers to entry that were developed. and see how they were overcome by Kodak, IBM, and the Japanese firms.
3. See the risks of a strong monopolistic position and of a diversification move.
4. Understand tradeoffs such as high performance vs. low cost and high reliability.
5. Understand the role of competitor analysis.
6. See alternative entry strategies of foreign competitors.
7. Assess assets and skills of a firm.

The following provide an overview of the industry that the students should understand:

1960's:	Xerox dominates and creates barriers.
1970's:	Xerox slept and was diverted. Market share fell from 96% to 46%.
1975:	Savin 750 enters under $5,000.
	Kodak Ektaprint 100 enters at high end.
1980:	Cannon NP-200 follows in 1983 with the PC-10.
1980's:	Xerox wakes up.

Questions for Discussion
1. Identify and evaluate Xerox strategy in the 1960's.
2. What entry barriers did Xerox create in the 1960's?
3. Identify and evaluate the strategy of IBM, Kodak, Ricoh/Savin, Cannon, and Minolta. How did each overcome barriers?
4. Why did Xerox lose position in 1970's?
5. What were the strengths and weaknesses of Xerox in 1980?
6. What should Xerox do to come back in the 1980's?

1. IDENTIFY AND EVALUATE XEROX STRATEGY IN THE 1960's

There are seven strategy elements that can be identified and discussed. Each of them represents a key Xerox strategic choice and was not obvious even in retrospect. For each, the students can be asked to identify the strategy rationale and to determine if they would have pursued a similar strategy.

Rented Equipment

The original product was complex and risky to customers, who certainly did not want to spend a lot of money on buying a machine. The decision to lease was absolutely brilliant and helped make Xerox what it is today. Who could resist $90 a month and only four cents a copy after the first free 2,000? What happened was that firms grossly underestimated the usage levels which averaged 8,000 per month. In 1967, the average Xerox 914 made 100,000 copies per month. In an original evaluation of the machine in 1960, A.D. Little estimated a total world market of only 5,000. A key assumption A. D. Little made was that the machine would be sold instead of leased.

Leasing reduced the risk to the customer, created entry barriers to competition and allowed Xerox to control the supplies business, which was a gold mine. It did, however, have disadvantages. It raised the financing requirements for Xerox and put less pressure from the customer upon reliability. Worse, it made the firm have a vested interest in keeping the old technology/machines. This aspect undoubtedly cost Xerox later.

Sales/Service Network

The machines were new to office management and continually broke down. Sales and service organizations were crucial to the strategy, and Xerox was strong in these areas from the start. However, these organizations were very costly for a firm that was struggling to finance the new product and its growth. The use of dealers or third party service organizations was an option that must have been attractive.

International--Joint Ventures

The commitment to joint ventures can be criticized. First, it sacrificed substantial profits--Xerox got only 50% of Europe and Latin America and 25% of the Far East. Second, their communication with Fuji Xerox was a big problem. Xerox did not foresee the importance of exploiting Fuji-Xerox product development nor could it understand the possibility of the future Japanese competitors. If Xerox had been in Japan itself, the communication might have been better. The Savin experience is also relevant to evaluating joint ventures

On the other hand, the joint ventures:
- allowed Xerox to move quickly into Europe and Japan, bypassing the organizational, financial (costs of setting up a service operation and financing the leases), and cultural hurdles.
- provided substantial success that may simply not have occurred any other way. Fuji-Xerox is often held forth as one of the U.S. success stories in Japan.
- provided autonomous product development.

Technology--Patents

A key was clearly the technology and the patents that surrounded it. The importance of the Xerox 914 technology cannot be overestimated. One Xerox executive said that "we were able to sell almost anything we made at whatever price we wanted to charge." The issue is how best to maintain that strength.

License CPC Technology

The decision to license CPC technology did provide an entry for firms that later became important competitors. Why? First, it was good money. Second, it may have diffused some of the anti-trust pressure. Third, the CPC technology was regarded by Xerox as obsolete.

Ignore Low End

The explicit decision to ignore the low end was fateful. In retrospect, a low end entry even if it was a money loser would have shut down a window of opportunity for other companies. In retrospect it seems dumb. However, at the time Xerox was stretched thin managing the growth despite their profitability and the money was clearly in the high end.

Diversification into the Office of the Future

A very reasonable diversification move. The problem is that it diverted attention from the main product. More on this under Question 4.

2. WHAT BARRIERS WERE CREATED BY XEROX BY 1970?

A market structure analysis (using Porter's framework) could be quickly done. It would show that Xerox was in an incredible monopoly position and would demonstrate why they were making a ton of money. The barriers were:

- Technology--Patents
- Capital Cost
   Lease Base
   Sales/Service System
- Xerox Name
- Global Presence

3. IDENTIFY AND EVALUATE THE STRATEGY OF IBM, KODAK, RICOH/SAVIN, CANNON AND MINOLTA. HOW DID EACH OVERCOME BARRIERS?

IBM

The IBM strategy was basically to build a me-too product and rely upon its sales/service operation and its name. The strategy really did not work. Xerox sued for patent infringement and basically won. IBM's inferior product meant that IBM dug itself into a hole from the beginning.

Kodak

The Kodak strategy was to attack the high end with a technologically superior product and to very slowly build an organization to support its product. Kodak explicitly decided to grow very slowly. As a result they developed a solid business. They were lucky in that they came out in 1975 expecting only a few years of superiority. They had, in fact, a window of over five years. Thus their slow approach didn't hurt them so much although it is clear that a more aggressive strategy would have enabled them to gain a much more dominant position. Some interesting questions to pose:

- What would have happened if IBM had the Kodak machine? (Xerox might have been killed.)
- Why did Kodak rather than IBM generate the best technology? Was it an accident? (Consider the technology behind Kodak. In fact most of the copier firms have photographic backgrounds.)
- Should Kodak have been more aggressive? (Given their culture, it is not clear an aggressive push was even feasible for them.)

Savin/Ricoh

The Savin 750, a reliable, 20 cps copier introduced for under $5,000 in 1975 was a bombshell. In had one-third the parts and weight of its Xerox competition and cost $500 to build. It had a 17,000 copies PR failure rate as compared to 6,000 for Xerox.

The technology barrier was overcome by the development of a new process that overcame the Xerox patents although their product came out 15 years after the 914. Could Xerox have pursued this technology and gotten patents on it as well? The problem is that unless you are driven by desperation, it is hard to exert the effort. It is rare that the market leader is the one that generates the new technologies.

The capital cost and sales/service system barriers were overcome by focusing upon reliability and cost and thus having a product that could be handled by dealers. The Xerox name was overcome by having dramatic price-performance superiority and the fact that they really didn't compete head-to-head against Xerox. The Savin team had perhaps a superior and more co-ordinated global presence than Xerox.

Canon

Most of the Savin strategy applies to Canon. There are some differences. Canon did not use joint ventures and they marketed under the Canon name everywhere. The results are instructive. They introduced a good product in the early 1970's which languished until the NP-200 came out in 1980. Their decision not to joint venture or otherwise use an established American and European name and organization clearly hurt them in the seventies. Further, the effort to develop a global product and a global business had to be done alone. It was expensive and took a long time. However, in the long run it might have paid off. The Savin\Ricoh combination got into trouble when competition heated up in the eighties. Ricoh decided they needed to get out from under the joint ventures to compete. Canon was in a very good position in the eighties.

Minolta

Minolta was forced by Ricoh and Canon to enter the PPC market in the late 1970s. They took a technology approach and attempted to create a better machine. Contrast that with the IBM me-too strategy.

4. WHY DID XEROX LOSE POSITION IN THE SEVENTIES?

Diverted by Office of the Future

Xerox rather logically felt in the sixties that they had no more worlds to conquer in copiers, so they looked for new growth directions. Building from the copier base they chose office-of-the-future, a logical expansion direction as it moved toward the customer system and seemed to be supported by environmental trends. Thus, they bought a host of component firms and a mainframe manufacturer and set up PARC (Palo Alto Research Center) which had some of the best computer people around; in fact, it developed the software that was to be the basis of the Apple Mac system.

However, the firm was not able to keep the excitement and attention on copiers. The action was in the office product systems. Further, the office products and all the computer entries were disappointing or failures. Thus, the organization diverted resources to build/save this area of the future.

Diverted by Anti-Trust Cases

The case documents how the firm got bogged down. The cost was not only the money and the time of the executives, but strategy options. Xerox had a tendency to be much less aggressive in pricing and product options. Prices were kept high which provided extra margins, but made it easier for the competition to come in.

Breakdown in Product Delivery System

The Xerox organization simply could not deliver new products. There were two main reasons. The first was organizational. A new product concept had to go to drafting (to get it drawn), to service (to see if it could be serviced), to manufacturing (to see if it could be made cheaply), and then to marketing. The process virtually made it impossible to move quickly and to pursue good ideas.

Second, the communication was terrible. Even though the PARC group could have provided key breakthroughs in microprocessor communication, they were not consulted. Instead, competing firms like Kodak and Minolta, solved the multiple microprocessor linkage problem in copiers. Xerox did not exploit what should have been substantial synergy.

The third was a preoccupation with speed and sophistication. Xerox wanted only to be fast, state of the art. Attributes of reliability and cost were not of any concern. Why? Probably because they were not close to either the customer or the competitors.

Arrogance About Xerox Technology

Xerox seemed to believe that they were the only ones that could make a copier that was sophisticated. The patents were the ultimate protection. There are several partial explanations:

- They did not do good competitor analysis if they did any. This despite the presence of Fuji-Xerox which was in an excellent position to learn of competitors and in fact tried to communicate with Xerox.
- They were a virtual monopoly until 1975 making incredible profits.

- They had a perception that the technology was extremely complex. They tended to use specially-made parts even for simple items such as screws. In contrast, the Japanese used as many standard parts as possible.

Turned Back On Low End

The President of Canon, replying to a question about what he would have done in 1970 to forestall the competition, said that it was easy: he would have entered the low end. Xerox saw that the very early Japanese machines didn't work well and wrote them off. They turned their back on some viable Fuji-Xerox options. Their own efforts were not successful.

Why? There are some logical reasons besides their focus upon speed, their technological arrogance, and their failure to do competitor analysis. First, the use of dealers would create problems with their sales force and customers. Second, they would cannibalize the rest of their lines and hurt some very profitable products. Third, they would obsolete the lease base.

5. WHAT WERE STRENGTHS AND WEAKNESSES OF XEROX IN 1980?

Strengths--
- Strong position in high-volume segment
- Large installed base
- Name
- Sales/service network
- Global presence
- Wide product line
- Some electronics capabilities

Weaknesses
- High manufacturing costs
- Weak low-volume segment
- Low reliability
- Office automation position unclear

6. WHAT SHOULD XEROX DO TO COME BACK IN THE 1980's?

There are a variety of things that Xerox did starting in 1979 to turn things around and become competitive. They included the following seven strategies:

1. **Competitive benchmarking**. Xerox became serious about competitor analysis. They got good information about competitor's costs and performance and projected them forward. They even benchmarked against non-competitors (such as the warehouse system of L.L. Bean) that did well in some aspect of their business.

2. **Low cost goals**. Xerox developed cost goals so that it would be competitive with the Japanese. That meant in part that reliability and cost increased in their priorities. One aspect of cost control was a reduction of staff so that the overhead was reduced. By

1985 their overhead had been reduced from $500 million to $275 million and direct labor was only 10% of the cost. The parts inventory dropped from 3.3 months to 1.0 months.

3. **Product quality goals**. Xerox developed quantitative quality goals and dramatically improved quality. Their defects per machine in the 10 series was 65% of former products. A total organizational commitment to quality was initiated.

4. **New product development**. Xerox re-organized the new product development effort so that the process was streamlined and much faster. Teams of people now had responsibility for a new product development cycle. One product that took from $1,000 to $1,500 million and seven years would not take more than $300 million and four years.

5. **Market research**. Paying much closer attention to the customer was evidenced by formal marketing research, more concept tests, use tests, customer observations, surveys, etc.

6. **Internationalization**. Xerox attempted to turn the international presence into more of an asset by improving the co-ordination between the Xerox, Fuji-Xerox and Rank-Xerox and using world-wide sourcing.

7. **A new product line**, the 10 series, which was first shipped in volume in 1983, was a key to the turnaround. It provided a technological advance that finally regained the technology position for Xerox. It used nine microprocessor brains to control quality and the processing. It had an advanced recirculating document handler and organic photorecepter which allowed the machine to be more compact.

The program worked in that the long steep slide in share was reversed and, in 1983, share actually went up two or three points. A Minolta executive was quoted as saying that "It appeared that we could kill Xerox too. Now I don't think so. Japanese people don't talk about it but Xerox is taking more and more market share back."

CONCLUSION

In summary, the case brings home a number of points--

1. The long-term importance of the strategic decisions to lease, to avoid the low end, to go for product sophistication, and to use joint ventures.

2. The arrogance of success/monopoly and the risk of diversification.

3. The risks to the country of anti-trust enforcement. Without the anti-trust efforts, the Japanese may not have ever arrived. Certainly this is arguable.

4. The importance of organizational communication and structure.

5. The variety of ways of approaching global competition.

6. The importance of competitor analysis.

7. How entry barriers can be created and by-passed.

SECTION 12

INTEL CASE

Intel was founded in 1968 by Gordon E. Moore and the late Robert N. Noyce, who in 1957 invented a form of the integrated circuit. The firm was an early leader in DRAM or dynamic random access memory. In 1971, it invented the microprocessor which ultimately won IBM's approval and became the industry standard. The chip that powered the first 1981 vintage IBM PC was called the 8086. The X86 family now includes:

-the 286 introduced in 1982
-the 386 introduced in 1985
-the 486 introduced in 1989.

The X86 name was extensively used by computer manufacturers in their naming strategy. Many computer manufacturers, for example, would use 486 or 4 in their product names to communicate to the customers exactly what microprocessor was inside. The name also served to imply that the software would be backward compatible with computers that used prior X86 microprocessors. The Dell product line included:

-Dell Dimension 386SX/25 (386SX running at 25 MHz)
-Dell 386/25 (386 running at 25 MHz)
-Dell 486D/20 (486 running at 20 MHz)
-Dell PowerLine 450DE (486 running at 50 MHz),

The COMPAQ line included:

-COMPAQ Prolinea 4/33 (486 running at 33 MHz)
-COMPAQ DESKPRO/i486/33 (Intel 486 running at 33 MHz)

In 1989, Intel had sales of $3.1 billion of which $1.2 billion was in microprocessors. In 1992, sales were projected to reach $5.5 billion with $3.1 billion in microprocessors. The firm in 1992 also made other chips ($1.4 billion), memory flash memory ($200 million), PC enhancement products ($380 million), and computers ($530 million). Profits in 1992 were projected to be around $800 million, of which microprocessors generated more than their proportionate share.

In the 1992 annual meeting Dr. Craig Barrett, Intel's executive vice-president, noted that the Intel strategy has been and continues to be based upon five key assets and skills. The first is Intel's silicon technology capability which has enabled Intel to increase transistor counts and improve production efficiency. The second is the X86 architecture which has become an industry standard. In the early 1990s, the X86 standard commanded around 85% of the PC and workstation market. Motorola had most of the balance while chips using RISC architecture had a share that was not much over 1%. More operating systems were based on the Intel X86 architecture than any other. The third, the design technology capability, allowed Intel to increase the microprocessor power and to introduce product derivatives. In 1992 over 30 different products such as speed doublers and three volt devices were planned to be offered in response to customer requests. The fourth is customer service. The Intel goal was to be rated "excellent" by customers and thus to achieve a reputation as being superior on this dimension. Employee compensation was tied to corporate performance in this area. The fifth was the recognition of the Intel and Intel Inside brand names.

In early 1991, Intel was experiencing competitive pressure. Advanced Micro Devices was already on the market (by the summer it had 15% of the PC market) with its AMD386DX chip clone. On the horizon was Chips and Technologies which was expected to announce a family of 386 clones in the Fall of 1991. Unfortunately, Intel did not obtain trademark protection on the X86 series and thus competitors were free to use 386 in their brand names. The products of these firms often differed from that of Intel's. In fact, AMD's strategy was to hold the price but to offer more features and performance than the Intel versions. Similarly, Chips and Technology's chip was 10% faster than Intel's. The result was customer confusion as to what exactly the 386 label meant.

To respond to the competitor pressure and customer confusion, Intel in the Spring of 1991 begin the "Intel Inside" program. It was aimed at creating a PC-user preference for PCs with Intel-based microprocessors, especially the 386 series. The program involved Intel advertising and the support of the advertising of computer firms willing to use the "Intel Inside" logo. In 1991 the logo appeared on approximately 3,000 pages of the advertising of computer firms. This number was estimated to grow to over 5,000 pages in 1992. In 1992, Intel budgeted around $100 million for the campaign. The campaign actually originated in Japan where Matsushita used it as a way to gain a hi-tech credibility for its computers. Japan is a country in which the prestige and visibility of corporate names is extremely important.

The "Intel Inside" program was not without its difficulties.

First, there was some resistance. For example, COMPAQ initially felt that the logo would inhibit its own image as being different from the clones--they later decided to add the logo.

Second, there was potential confusion about what "Intel Inside" meant. The logo obviously referred to microprocessors such as the 386 and the 486. However, Intel also made a host of products that went inside the computer such as fax boards, modem boards, multimedia components, math co-processors, and network components. Would these items be helped or hurt by "Intel Inside," which refers to microprocessors? Might not consumers assume that Intel made only microprocessors?

Third, the name Intel refers both to a corporation and to branded products, namely microprocessors and many others. Does that cause confusion? Intel as a corporation means a large reliable firm that will not disappear or create new microprocessors that will obsolete your old ones. What should Intel mean as a product rather than a corporation?

Fourth, how should the program be judged? With respect to awareness it seemed to be doing its job. However, how it should be evaluated was unclear.

In the Fall of 1992, Intel was ready to announce the "586" chip which represented a significant performance advance over the 486 chip. One option was to call it i586 or Intel 586. That would build upon the X86 equity that had been developed and would fit with the "Intel Inside" thrust. Customers were certainly expecting a 586 generation and understood generally what it meant.

Intel, however, selected the second option: to create a new brand name. The logic was that a new name would be required to regain control of the Intel microprocessor. In addition to confusion as to what a 386 was, some competitors were labeling as 486 products that were really 386. It seemed likely that they would label as 586 products that were really 486. The customer confusion would thus increase and the brand equity of Intel and its OEMs would be affected. As a result, customers would increasingly be unable to discern genuine Intel-based systems. There was no way for Intel to prevent this abuse of the X86 naming scheme. A new name that was trademarkable would be controlled by Intel and would enable them to create equity for Intel and its OEM customers that would be protected.

Candidate names were obtained from customers, Intel employees, and naming firms. The name that was selected from over 3,500 possibilities was Pentium, which has, at least to some, the connotation of fifth generation.

One of Intel's goals was to protect the new name so that it would not also be lost. Toward that end the following guidelines were put into place--

Never use the trademark as a plural or verb
    Wrong--Use Newchips to enhance your software.
    Wrong--Newchip your computer
Usage in OEM system names is not permitted
    Wrong--The CMC Newchip 500
OEMs may reference inclusion of Newchip CPU
    Right--The CMC 550 contains the Intel Newchip microprocessor.
ISVs may reference software applicability for Newchip CUU
    Wrong--Newchip Funsheet
    Right--Funsheet for Newchip CPU based computers

Questions for discussion:

1. In the Spring of 1991 the Intel Inside campaigning was started, and $100 million was budgeted in 1992. Was that worthwhile? Why would COMPAQ participate in the program? Dell? How would you evaluate it?

2. In the Fall of 1992, the "586" chip was ready. Would you call it Intel 586 or i586 or would you start over with a new name? What are the pros and cons of each alternative?

3. Assume a new name alternative was desired. What criteria for a new name would you develop? Evaluate Pentium with respect to these criteria.

4. How would you introduce the new name?

5. In 1989, how much would you have paid for the rights to the X86 name? How would you structure an analysis to generate a defensible number?

Written by David Aaker, Haas School of Business, 1992.

SECTION 13

TEACHING NOTES: INTEL CASE

1. In the Spring of 1991 the Intel Inside campaign was started, and $100 million was budgeted in 1992. Was that worthwhile? How would you evaluate it? Why would Compaq or Dell participate?

What were the problems facing Intel?

1. Competitors were selling the Intel name 386/486
2. Competitors were distorting it by selling different versions than Intel, even to the point of labeling as 486 what was really 386.
3. Losing control not only of the name but also the product.

Was the $100-million campaign worthwhile?

NO it was a mistake--spend $100 million on R&D or shareholders
- OEMs just buy on price and specs and you need to compete on price and specs.
- end users just buy a 386 class machine from Compaq and don't care what chip is used.
   If so it makes no sense--you hurt your cost structure--better spend on R&D
   What about Nutrasweet--was their campaign effective? They insisted that all use their logo.

YES it was a good move
- It works by making people more familiar with Intel--people are reassured by the Intel name even though they have no clue as to how it differs--Why look into it - just buy Intel and be sure.
- Q exactly how.
- Intel gets the endorsement of IBM Compaq etc.
- There must be a reason that Intel is placed there--must be quality.
- Intel name means reliability, backward-compatible.
- In fact, there was a much higher incidence of buyers who spec'd Intel.

Note: What about the logo? Isn't it friendly?

Note: Compare the effectiveness of Intel Inside vs. a campaign telling people that Intel is better because of a dozen factual reasons. If you try to communicate a perspective that makes Intel look better, AMD will find another in which

127

they are better and, as with aspirin, people will assume that all are same. Intel Inside is much harder to compete against.

Note: Intel Inside was really the idea of Dentsu who was trying to do something to make Intel better known and more prestigious in Japan.

How to measure the results of Intel Inside
- Measure the space advertising--
  During 18 months (1992 and first half of 1993), over 90,000 pages of OEM ads contained the Intel Inside Logo. If each page is seen by 100,000 people that is 10 billion impressions.
- Measure the awareness
  Recognized the brand (exact task unknown)

	Nutrasweet	1992(when unknown)	1993
PC specifies (Job to specify)	80%	60%	90%
Business end users	80%	46%	80%

- Measure the extra people will pay
- Measure the market share/price
- Measure the attitude toward
- Measure the image of Intel

Why would Compaq or Dell participate?
1. To avoid being perceived as less than others on the chip side
2. Because Intel pays for part of their ad and gives them access to their lowest advertising rate. Actually the OEMs get a 3 percent merchandising credit that can be used to pay for up to 50 percent of the OEMs space advertising. In addition, they get another 2% if they will put the Intel Inside Logo on the case and shipping container.

2. **In the Fall of 1992, the "586" chip was ready. Would you call it Intel 586 or i586 or would you start over with a new name? What are the pros and cons of each alternative?**

Pro for i586
- draws upon the X86 equity
   customers already know what the product is
- the Intel Inside provides a brand name that is Intel - you don't need another
- competitors will not be allowed to have the 586 name for nothing
- a new name will cost a bundle--
   does it really matter that much in customer choice?
- under a new name competitors will get 586 free

Con for i586
- competitors usurping--like a new chocolate company using Hershey, Intel doesn't own
- competitor game-playing generates confusion that Intel cannot control
- Intel can control and own a new name

3. Assume a new name alternative was desired. What criteria for a new name would you develop? Evaluate Pentium with respect to the new name.

Pentium should suggest fifth generation, an ingredient (radium etc.), and hi tech.

Intel's Criteria
Trademarkable
Hard to copy
Has positive associations
Works worldwide
Can effectively transition from generation to generation
Supports Intel's brand equity
Works with our partners' brand names

Secondary goals
Memorable
Sounds technically sophisticated
Suggests what the product is

Other possible goals
Associated with Intel
Associated with microprocessors

Some of the 3,500 names that were generated by task force, contest, and naming firms were:
> Tested with end users
> Subjected to Int'l trademark search and world-wide linguistic review

Funny: iCUCyrix, iAmFastest, 586NOT!

4. How would you introduce Pentium?

       Big splash
       Trade shows, advertising, OEMs
       Role of PR

5. In 1989, how much would you have paid for the rights to the X86 name? How would you structure an analysis to generate a defensible number?

It has to be compared to the alternative of creating a new name

a. Cost of new name
      Generate a name
            $35,000 from name lab alone
            test names
            qualify them internationally
      Communicate the name--create awareness
      Associate the name with the X86 series
      Associate the name with Intel
b. Reduction in sales due to loss of loyalty
      how much extra sales would you get if you kept X86
c. price premium times volume?

Measure the discount the world gives to buy a "non Intel" brand by regularly surveying people at COMPUSA and Fry's etc.--Gets at retail price in clone vs. Intel.

Because of its name (and perhaps because of its design), the new Apple Quantro appealed to business even though the guts were the same.

Written by David Aaker, Haas School of Business, October 1993.

SECTION 14

TEST QUESTIONS
for *Strategic Market Management*

Essay Questions

1. What is the objective of external analysis? How would you distinguish between an effective and ineffective external analysis? What would you say would be the most useful construct or method in an external analysis? Why?

2. Describe a growth option such as "penetration" (or diversification, product expansion or vertical integration). What are the advantages and disadvantages?

3. Discuss the advantages of a customizing rather than a standardizing marketing program in the context of a global strategy. When would customizing make sense?

4. Consider the implementation problems of merging Sears and Walt Disney. What synergy would you expect? How could you make sure that it materialized?

5. Describe scenario analysis using one of the cases discussed in the course as a vehicle to illustrate. What implementation problems would you expect if scenario analysis were to be adopted at Apple Computers?

6. American business has been accused of being short sighted, looking to the short term financial performance instead of taking a longer term view. What can a manager do to make sure that he or she is managing for the long term? How would you go about advising a department store to generate indicators of long-term success? Be specific.

7. Describe shareholder value analysis. What are the major problems in its implementation?

8. What are assumptions underlying the growth-share matrix? When are these assumptions likely to hold? What do you see as the appropriate role of the growth-share matrix?

9. What are the problems of implementing a preemptive move strategy? How could you maximize the chances of obtaining an SCA based upon a preemptive move?

10. Discuss the considerations involved in making the decision to expand or broaden the product line.

11. Describe the distinctions between strategic vision, strategic stubbornness, and strategic intent.

12. What are the six phases of hostility? How can you reduce the changes or chances that hostility will hit your market? How do you compete in a hostile market?

13. Describe and illustrate the following terms:
   -Scenario
   -Strategic uncertainties
   -Cross-impact analysis
   -Synergy
   -Strategic opportunism
   -Strategic drift
   -Key success factors
   -Experience curve
   -Borderless organization

Objective Questions

Note--These objective questions cover the book. In general, a false answer is markedly at odds with material in the book. However, it may not be at odds with other written material. Thus, it is important to position these questions as a test of a student's competence with the book material.

Preface
The development, evaluation, and implementation of business strategies are essential to successful management. The key is a management system that will help managers do all but one of the following:
   (a) monitor and understand a dynamic environment
   (b) provide vision to their business
   (c) guarantee reduced competition
   (d) generate strategic options that will be responsive to changes facing a business
   (e) develop strategies based on sustainable competitive advantages.

1.1 [p.6] (T)
When multiple businesses are involved, a business strategy should include six dimensions, one of which is the synergistic effects across the business units within the firm that will be exploited by the strategy.

1.2 [p. 7] (F)
A focus strategy is an alternative to a differentiation strategy--you would not have both.

1.3 [p. 9] (F)
A long-range planning system assumes that past extrapolations are inadequate, that new trends and discontinuities will occur that require strategic adjustments.

1.4 [p. 8] (F)
A strategic market management system will have more value for an organization that is not engaged in complex markets with multiple channels and regional variation in channels and products.

1.5 [p. 9](T)
The six elements of strategy can be capsuled into three core elements--the product-market investment decision, functional area strategies, and the basis of a sustainable competitive advantage.

1.6 [p. 8] (F)
A strategic business unit (SBU) is any organizational unit that has a defined business strategy, a manager with sales and profit responsibility, and a strategic planner who is responsible to put together the company's annual strategic marketing plan.

1.7 [p. 8] (B)
Despite the costs and problems, strategic marketing management has the potential to do all except one of the following:
    (a) precipitate the consideration of strategic choices.
    (b) guarantee the success of the SBU.
    (c) force a long-range view.
    (d) make visible the resource allocation decision.
    (e) provide methods to help strategic analysis and decision-making.

1.8 [p. 6] (the level of investment for each product-market area, the assets or competencies which provide the basis for SCA, and the specification of synergy expected.)

The six elements of a business strategy for a firm with multiple business units are the product-market specification, the functional area strategies, the allocation of resources over the business units, _____, _____, and _____.

1.9 [p. 9] (D)

From a historical perspective there are four terms that have defined strategic marketing. Which of the following is not one of them?

     (a) Strategic market management
     (b) Long-range planning
     (c) strategic planning
     (d) strategic prognosticating
     (e) Budgeting/control

1.10 [p.18] (T)

Most strategies have either a differentiation or low-cost strategic thrust, or both.

1.11 (F)

The need for strategic analysis and decision making always occurs right at the close of the fiscal year and it is not always possible to plan strategies at that time.

1.12 (E)

Strategic marketing is involved in making decisions, some of which include investment decisions. Of the following which is not an investment decision:

     (a) invest for growth
     (b) milk
     (c) maintain
     (d) liquidate
     (e) differentiation

1.13 (T)

A proactive strategy attempts to influence events in the environment rather than simply react to environmental forces as they occur.

2.1 [p. 23](F)

An external analysis includes the analysis of the customers, the competitors, the distribution channels and the environment.

2.2 [p. 26] (T)
An opportunity is a trend or event that could lead to a significant upward change in sales and profit patterns given the appropriate strategic response.

2.3 [p. 30] (F)
Among the five criteria that should be used in selecting strategies is that a strategy should maximize profits.

2.4 [p. 34] (F)
The strategy development process which involves external analysis, internal analysis, identifying strategic options, selecting a strategy, and implementation should ideally be sequential.

2.5 [p. 27] (F)
A strategic vision is a vision of the external environment in the future.

2.6 [p. 30] (involving a sustainable competitive advantage, being feasible and being consistent with organizational vision/objectives)
The criteria for selecting strategies include considering the relationship to other firm strategies, considering scenarios, _____, _____, and _____.

2.7 [p. 28] (core values, core purpose, BHAGs)
A vision for a business should include three components _____, _____, and _____.

2.8 [p. 24] (B)
Environmental analysis can be divided into five components. Which of the following is not one of those components:
    (a) demographic
    (b) psychographic
    (c) economic
    (d) cultural
    (e) governmental

2.9 [p. 23] (F)
A key success factor is a competitive asset or competency that gives a company a competitive advantage.

2.10 [p. 21] (E)
To develop a strategy, it is important to understand all of the following criteria about your competitor except:

     (a) strengths and weaknesses
     (b) objectives
     (c) current and past strategy
     (d) cost structure
     (e) national unemployment rate

2.11 [p. 20] (T)
Customer analysis involves identifying the organization's customer segments and each segment's motivations and unmet needs.

2.12 [p. 18] (T)
Strategic market management is a system designed to help management both precipitate and make strategic decisions, as well as create strategic visions.

2.13 [p. 25] (B)
Non-financial performance measures that often provide better measures of long-term business health include all but one of the following:

     (a) manager/employee capability and performance
     (b) return on assets
     (c) brand/firm association
     (d) customer satisfaction/brand loyalty
     (e) product/service quality

2.14 [p. 30] (C)
Internal analysis includes all but one of the following:

     (a) internal examination.
     (b) organizational structure.
     (c) leading economic indicators
     (d) organizational systems.
     (e) people and culture.

2.15 [p.23] (F)
Key success factors are those factors that a company performs better than all of their competitors.

2.16 [p. 19] (B)
External analysis is divided into four sections. Which of the following is not one of those sections?
- (a) environmental analysis
- (b) cost analysis
- (c) customer analysis
- (d) market analysis
- (e) competitor analysis

3.1 [p. 41] (F)
A strategic uncertainty identifies the most important strategic options.

3.2 [p. 44](T)
An external analysis should be part of the annual planning exercise but should not be restricted to that role.

3.3 [p. 47] (F)
Benefit segmentation is a segmentation scheme based upon an evaluation of the benefits to the firm provided by various segments.

3.4 [p. 55]((F)
Lead users are product users that use more of a product category than other users.

3.5 (F)
A good objective for an external analysis is to generate a comprehensive descriptive study of an industry.

3.6 [p. 50] (T)
In determining consumer motivations, individual interviews are generally more cost effective than group interviews.

3.7 [p. 53] (unmet needs)
A customer analysis consists of three components; segmentation, customer motivation, and _____.

3.8 (scenario analysis)
Uncertainty can be handled by making a strategic decision, by obtaining information to reduce the uncertainty, and by _____.

3.9 (D)

Understanding competitors and their activities can provide several benefits. These include all but one of the following:

    (a) insight into future competitor strategies may allow the prediction of emerging threats and opportunities.

    (b) a decision about strategic alternatives might easily hinge on the ability to forecast likely reactions of key competitors.

    (c) it might result in identification of some strategic uncertainties.

    (d) it will provide you a tool to determine your return on investment.

    (e) understanding their strengths and weaknesses can suggest opportunities that will merit a response.

4.1 [p. 61] (T)

One way to identify competitors is to determine what competitive brands are used in the same use situation by actual customers.

4.2 [p. 61] (F)

A strategic group is a customer segment that is strategically important to the business.

4.3 (T)

The dimensions of competitor analysis should include objectives and assumptions.

4.4 [p. 68] (T)

Mobility barriers are barriers inhibiting the movement from one strategic group to another. They reflect both exit and entry barriers.

4.5 [p. 75] (F)

The competitive strength grid lists the product markets served by each competitor and identifies for each product market the strengths of each competitor.

4.6 [p. 70] (F)

The value chain analysis is based upon the cost-benefit of the product as perceived by the customer.

4.7 [p. 65] (image and positioning, strengths & weaknesses, and organization & culture)

The eight dimensions of competitor analysis include "current & past strategies," "cost structure", "exit barriers," "objectives and assumptions," "size, growth and profitability," _____, _____, and _____.

4.8 (A)
In conducting a competitor analysis, which of the following is not relevant:
     (a) accounting methodologies
     (b) market share
     (c) image
     (d) positioning strategy
     (e) objectives and commitments

4.9 [p. 68] (D)
Exit barriers are crucial to a firm's ability to exercise an exit alternative. Which of the following is not an exit barrier?
     (a) managerial pride
     (b) government or social barriers
     (c) specialized assets
     (d) high market growth rate
     (e) fixed costs

4.10 [p. 72] (E)
In completing a checklist on competitor assets and competencies, some of the areas to be considered include all but one of the following:
     (a) company culture
     (b) innovation
     (c) manufacturing
     (d) management
     (e) strategic programming

4.11 [p. 64] (D)
In addition to current competitors, it is important to consider potential market entrants such as firms that might engage in all but one of the following:
     (a) retaliatory or defensive strategies
     (b) market expansion
     (c) forward integration
     (d) price fixing
     (e) backward integration

4.12 (F)
Environmental analysis is the least important factor in external analysis.

4.13 [p. 64] (B)
Potential market entrants might use all but one of the following to enter a market:

    (a) market expansion

    (b) market penetration

    (c) product expansion

    (d) backward/forward integration

    (e) export assets or competencies

4.14 [p. 61] (E)
Some of the benefits of strategic groups include all but one of the following:

    (a) Makes the process of competitor analysis more manageable.

    (b) Refines the strategic investment decision.

    (c) Includes a set of mobility barriers.

    (d) They will be affected by and react to industry developments in similar ways.

    (e) They produce strategic directions

4.15 [p. 66] (T)
In order to develop positioning alternatives, it is helpful to determine the image and brand personality of the major competitors.

5.1 [p. 80] (F)
A usage gap is caused when one segment uses more of a product than another segment.

5.2 (F)
The goal of strategy development is to identify growth areas and invest in them and to identify declining areas and disinvest in them.

5.3 (T)
An analysis of the industry structure provides insight into the present and future profitability of an industry.

5.4 [p. 78] (T)
Key success factors are assets or competencies that are necessary for a firm to be successful in an industry.

5.5 [p. 92] (T)
The biggest risk of high growth contexts is the fact that the number of competitors attracted is likely to be high.

5.6 [p. 87] (T)
Avoiding small niche markets can risk being late into a growth situation.

5.7 [p. 96] (substitute products, bargaining power of suppliers, and bargaining power of customers.)
An industry structure analysis involves five components--the intensity of competition, pressure from potential competitors, _____, _____, and _____.

6.1 [p. 99] (F)
One of the five components of environmental analysis is life style.

6.2 [p. 102] (T)
Information technology is the basis for a key sustainable competitive advantage for Levi Strauss.

6.3 [p. 104] (T)
Working women are not much more convenience oriented in food purchasing than non-working women. They do not tend to be heavier users of such convenience products as packaged cookies, frozen pizza, and cake mix.

6.4 [p. 106] (T)
Cross impact analysis involves determining the impact of one event on the probability of another.

6.5 [p. 111] (F)
The ideal number of scenarios to work with is three to five.

6.6 [p. 108] (T)
A strategic uncertainty should be evaluated with respect to its impact and immediacy.

6.7 [p. 99] (culture, and demographics)
The five components of environmental analysis are technology, government, economics, _____, and _____.

7.1 [p. 118] (F)
A study of the corporate objectives of 82 large firms showed that the objective used by the highest percentage of firms was product quality and service.

7.2 [p. 118] (T)
ROA is return on sales times asset turnover.

7.3 [p. 135] (T)
Book assets is usually a distorted measure of assets employed.

7.4 [p. 119] (T)
According to Hayes and Garvin, American firms have excessive hurdle rates because they tend to use a common hurdle rate for all projects.

7.5 [p. 129] (T)
If the net present value of future cash flows generated by a business investment is positive, than the business is creating shareholder value.

7.6 [p. 115] (T)
Shareholder value analysis focuses attention on numbers and away from strategy.

7.7 [p. 115] (T)
Shareholder value analysis provides a long-term perspective and a way to avoid an over-reliance on short - term financials.

7.8 [p. 115] (F)
The most important objective priority for Japanese firms is to achieve high product quality.

7.9 [p. 119] (T)
Economic value added takes into account the capital employed in the business and the cost of capital.

7.10 [p. 126] (Benchmarking)
_____ is comparing the performance of a business component such as warehouse operations with similar operations in other companies.

7.11 [p. 115] (T)
A business internal analysis is similar to a competitor analysis, but it has a greater focus on performance assessments.

7.12 [p. 122] (A)

Performance measures reflecting long-term profitability include all but one of the following:
- (a) using robotics for production
- (b) product/service quality
- (c) customer satisfaction
- (d) new product activity
- (e) relative cost

7.13 [p.122] (T)

Perhaps one of the more important assets of many firms is the loyalty of the customer.

7.14 [p. 126] (C)

Determinants of strategic options and choices consist of all but one of the following:
- (a) strengths/weaknesses
- (b) organizational capabilities/constraints
- (c) marketing myopia
- (d) strategic problems
- (e) past and current strategies

7.15 [p.145] (T)

In internal analysis, organizational strengths and weaknesses need to be not only identified but also related to competitors and the market.

8.1 [p. 142] (T)

Among the critical determinants of a SCA is the choice of the product market and the identity and nature of competitors.

8.2 [p. 142] (F)

An effective sustainable competitive advantage should be substantial enough to matter, be sustainable, be different from competitors, and should involve synergy.

8.3 [p. 144] (T)

In the survey of 248 West Coast business managers, the most frequently mentioned SCA was a quality reputation.

8.4 [p. 146] (T)
Among the strategic thrusts that are available to a business are differentiation, low cost, focus, preemptive and synergistic.

8.5 [p. 147] (F)
When synergy is obtained you find that two businesses have lower operating costs when operating together than they would have operating separately.

8.6 [p. 147] (T)
If two businesses have synergy, their profitability operating together will be higher than if they operated separately.

8.7 [p. 147] (F)
Synergy will result in one or more of the following: decreased revenues, increased operating costs or increased investment.

8.8 [p. 148] (T)
A core asset or competency is a firm asset or compentency that is capable of being the competitive basis of many of its businesses.

8.9 [p. 149] (F)
Strategic vision has been shown to be superior to strategic opportunism.

8.10 [p. 157] (T)
Strategic intent is a sustained obsession with winning which involves a stretch of the organization and real innovation.

8.11 [p. 150] (F)
A organization implementing a strategic vision should have an on-line information system and be capable of fast response.

8.12 [p. 158] (T)
Strategic drift is associated with an orientation toward the present.

8.13 [p. 150] (Buy-in throughout the organization, patience)
To successfully manage a strategic vision, a firm should have four characteristics--a clear future strategy, the needed assets and competencies, _____, and _____.

8.14 [p. 159] (investment in underused resources)
Strategic flexibility can be obtained by diversification, _____, and by reducing commitment of resources to a specialized use.

8.15 [p.149] (A)
To successfully manage a strategic vision, a firm should have four characteristics. Which of the following is not one of the four?
      (a) senior management with MBAs
      (b) buy-in throughout the organization
      (c) assets, competencies, and resources to implement it
      (d) patience
      (e) a clear future strategy

8.16 [p.146] (F)
A preemptive strategic move is an implementation of a strategy new to a business that generates an asset or competency that allows followers to either duplicate or at least respond easily to the strategy.

8.17 [p.143] (E)
A sustainable competitive advantage has several characteristics. Which of the following is not one of them:
      (a) their sustainability
      (b) they can be leveraged
      (c) they should be supported by assets and competencies
      (d) cannot easily be neutralized by competitors
      (e) they are easily copied

8.18 [p. 147] (T)
Synergy between SBUs can provide an SCA that is truly sustainable because it is based on the characteristics of a firm that are probably unique.

8.19 [p. 158] (D)
A firm should have four characteristics to successfully manage a strategic vision. Which of the following is not one of those characteristics?
      (a) Patience
      (b) Buy-in throughout the organization
      (c) Assets, competencies, and resources to implement the strategy
      (d) A drive to create immediate profits
      (e) A clear future strategy

8.20 [p. 142] (D)

Four factors are required for the creation of a sustainable competitive advantage. Which of the following is not one of those factors?

(a) Whom you compete against

(b) Basis of competition

(c) Where you compete

(d) Your strategic intent

(e) The way you compete

8.21 [p. 147] (B)

An SCA should have all but one of the following characteristics:

(a) be substantial

(b) be standardized

(c) should be employed against competitors who cannot easily match or neutralize the SCA

(d) segments will value the strategy

(e) supported by assets and competencies

8.22 [p.147] (T)

The key to strategic management can be the management of core assets and competencies rather than business units.

8.23 [p.146] (T)

A successful differentiation strategy will provide customers with value that is difficult for competitors to copy.

8.24 [p. 159] (C)

In developing strategies, it is useful to consider all except one of the following concepts:

(a) strategic flexibility

(b) strategic stubbornness

(c) who came up with the strategy

(d) strategic vision

(e) strategic opportunism

9.1 [p. 167] (T)

The definition of quality keeps changing in the automobile industry.

9.2 [p. 170] (T)
PIMS research indicates that businesses whose products have high perceived quality tended to have higher market share, higher prices and higher ROI.

9.3 [p. 172] (F)
Schlitz recovered from its product problems only after an expensive advertising campaign.

9.4 [p. 171] (T)
Perceived quality has been shown to affect stock return.

9.5 [p. 169] (T)
A quality strategy based upon superior quality is not enough--a firm must also manage the quality cues.

9.6 [p. 174] (T)
The Datsun name was just as strong as the Nissan name four years after the name change.

9.7 [p. 169] (T)
It has been shown empirically that a customer orientation is associated with higher profits.

9.8 [p. 173] (T)
Brand equity is a set of assets and liabilities that add to or subtract from the value provided by a product or service to the customers or to the firm.

9.9 [p. 166] (be difficult to copy)
A successful differentiation strategy should generate customer value, provide perceived value, and _____.

9.10 [p. 169] (tangibles)
The five service quality dimensions include reliability, responsiveness, competence, empathy and _____.

9.11 [p. 173] (brand loyalty, perceived quality)
The four dimensions of brand equity are awareness, identity, _____, and _____.

9.12 [p.164] (D)
Successful differentiation strategies should have several characteristics. Which of the following is not a characteristic of successful differentiation strategies?
 (a) developed from the customer's perspective
 (b) provides perceived value
 (c) difficult to copy
 (d) developed from the perspective of the business operation
 (e) generates customer value

9.13 [p. 166](T)
Most successful strategies will involve the total organization, its structure, systems, people and culture.

10.1 [p. 188] (T)
Under an experience curve the total cost of a product will decline at a predictable rate as experience in building the product accumulates.

10.2 [p. 188] (T)
One cause of the experience curve effect is product redesign.

10.3 [p. 188] (T)
To pursue an experience curve based strategy, it is crucial to have the largest share.

10.4 [p. 188] (F)
An experience curve strategy will usually enhance product innovation.

10.5 [p. 189] (F)
A low cost strategy will involve the experience curve.

10.6 [p. 190] (T)
A focus strategy will involve either differentiation or low cost.

10.7 [p. 191] (T)
A focus strategy can be used to bypass industry key success factors.

10.8 [p. 194] (F)
A preemptive move is defined to be the introduction of a new product or service into the market.

10.9 [p. 189] (T)
In computers, diet colas, and VCRs, the first entrants lost out to competitors that entered later.

10.10 [p. 196] (T)
When a preemptive move works, the competitors are inhibited from responding.

10.11 [p. 200] (synergy, the preemptive move)
The five strategic thrusts are differentiation, focus, low cost, _____, and _____.

10.12 [p. 182]   (no-frills product/service, scale economies)
The five approaches to a low-cost strategy are experience curve, production/operations, product design, _____ and _____.

10.13 [p. 182] (C)
The low-cost strategic thrust consists of all of the approaches below except:
        (a) scale economies
        (b) no-frills product/service
        (c) delivery of superior customer service
        (d) production/operations
        (e) experience curve

10.14 [p. 191] (D)
Focus strategies provide for all but one of the following:
        (a) avoid diluting or distracting strategy implementation
        (b) provide for a way to compete with limited resources
        (c) bypass assets and competencies of larger competitors
        (d) access to broad product markets
        (e) provide positioning strategy

11.1[p. 210] (F)
Yamaha responded to their Korean competition by developing a cost containment program which involved the off-shore manufacturing of key components.

11.2 [p. 212] (F)
The concept of obtaining synergies in financial services by combining firms like Dean Witter and Sears has proven successful largely because of the cross-selling that has occurred.

11.3 [p. 218] (F)
Among the benefits of vertical integration is a reduction in risk.

11.4 [p.215] (T)
Whenever only one buyer and one seller exist for highly specialized products and services, there will be an incentive to consider vertical integration.

11.5 [p. 220](F)
The most profitable firms tend to have neither a high nor a low degree of vertical integration.

11.6 [p.205] (finding new applications)
Product usage can be increased by increasing usage levels, increasing usage frequency, and _____.

12.1 [p. 222] (T)
Strategies of product expansion or market expansion are routes to diversification.

12.2 [p. 223] (F)
Vertical integration would usually be considered a diversification.

12.3 [p. 228] (T)
A related diversification involves commonalities that generate economies of scale or synergies based upon the exchange of competencies or resources.

12.4 [p. 228] (T)
A brand extension can be handicapped by a brand's negative attribute associations.

12.5 [p. 225] (T)
A brand extension can help the brand name in its original context.

12.6 [p. 231] (F)
Finance theory has shown that unrelated diversification will reduce the risk facing the business and thus be valued by stockholders.

12.7 [p. 231] (T)
The objectives of unrelated diversification are mainly financial such as to obtain a bargain price for a new business or to obtain liquid assets or cash flow.

12.8 [p. 233](F)
Studies have shown that diversified firms are generally more profitable than other firms.

12.9 (T)
A joint venture is recommended when either the market or the technology is unfamiliar.

12.10 [p. 224] (perceived quality associations)
The four association types that are often relevant in making brand extension decisions are attribute associations which are positive in the new context, attribute associations negative in the new context, product class associations and

_____.

12.11 [p.228] (planned synergy simply doesn't exist)
Related diversification can be risky because potential synergy is never realized because of implementation problems, because of antitrust laws and because

_____.

12.12 [p. 222] (T)
Diversification is the strategy of entering product markets different from those in which the firm is currently engaged.

13.1 [p.242](T)
One alternative in a declining market is to create a growth context by turning the declining industry into a growth industry.

13.2 [p. 243](F)
To be the profitable survivor in a declining industry it is important to avoid having competitors learn of your intentions.

13.3 [p. 243] (F)
A milk or harvest strategy avoids growth-motivated investment and aims to invest only that needed to maintain a firm's position.

13.4 [p. 243] (F)
A milk strategy may not work when the business is central to the current strategy of the firm.

13.5 [p. 244] (T)
The invest decision--hold, milk or exit--should be based upon an analysis of (1) the market prospects, (2) the competitive intensity, (3) the business strengths and performance, (4) the interrelationship of the business with other businesses of the firm, and (5) the implementation barriers.

13.6 [p. 250] (T)
One of the phases of hostility is entrance by multinational players.

13.7 (F)
In a hostile industry a Gold competitor tends to be a smaller firm who offers above-standard service and higher price points.

13.8 (specialized assets)
Exit barriers include long-term contract, commitments to provide spare parts and service backup, the impact upon the firm's reputation, and _____.

13.9 [p. 250] (self-defeating cost reduction, consolidation and shakeout, rescue)
The six phases of hostility are margin pressure, share shifts, product proliferation, _____, _____, and _____.

13.10 [p. 250] (C)
Hostile markets are those with all but one of the following:
    (a) overcapacity
    (b) intense competition
    (c) increasing demand
    (d) management in turmoil
    (e) low margins

14.1 [p. 255] (F)
A global strategy is a multinational strategy in which separate strategies are developed for different countries.

14.2 [p. 257] (T)
Among the eight motivations for global strategies is to cross-subsidize businesses and to obtain scale economies.

14.3 [p. 258] (T)
In the waterfall model, a firm first establishes itself in a domestic market.

14.4 [p. 258] (F)
The most important incentive for foreign investment among U.S. multinational firms is to obtain lower wage rates.

14.5 [p. 261] (T)
Strong motivations for a standardized global brand and position are media spillover and cross-country customer travel.

14.6 [p. 262] (F)
Kentucky Fried Chicken is a good example of global standardization--their operation in Japan, for example, is practically identical to that in the U.S.

14.7 [p. 261] (T)
The Takeuchi and Porter study of Japanese firms found that the brand name and advertising is likely to be standardized across countries.

14.8 [p. 259] (T)
One of the indicators that strategies should be global is--"major competitors in important markets are not domestic and have presence in several countries."

14.9 [p. 265] (F)
A lead country for a brand is where the firm is based.

14.10 [p. 266] (F)
Procter & Gamble's "Pampers experiment" in which a Pampers strategy was developed for the whole continent was successful largely because of the common advertising.

14.11 [p. 267] (F)
IBM has few strategic alliances in Japan.

14.12 [p. 269] (T)
The key to success of strategic alliances is to maintain strategic value for each of the participants.

14.13 [p. 268] (T)
A strategic alliance is commonly used to compensate for the absence of or weakness in any needed asset or competency.

14.14 [p. 257] (access strategic markets, obtain scale economies, access national incentives)
The seven motivations for global strategies are to cross-subsidize businesses, to dodge trade barriers, access low cost labor or materials, to create global associations, _____, _____, and _____.

15.1 [p. 228] (F)
One dimension of organizational structure is the budgeting system.

15.2 [p. 279] (F)
The borderless organization refers to the fact that global organizations need to function across borders and thus need to find ways to break down national boundaries.

15.3 [p. 280] (T)
The virtual corporation is a team of people and/or organizations formed for a particular client or job.

15.4 [p. 283] (T)
An organizational culture involves three elements; a set of "shared values", a set of norms of behavior, and a set of symbols and symbolic activities.

15.5 [p. 285] (T)
Because a culture is so hard to change, a strategy's fit with the organization's culture is of greater concern than the strategy's fit with other organization components.

15.6 [p. 289] (F)
In the hit industry model, pumpers operate best in a decentralized organization and generally involve marketing people.

15.7 [p.284](T)
According to O'Reilly norms can vary with respect to their intensity and with respect to the degree of consensus or consistency with which they are shared.

15.8 [p. 286] (T)
The achievement of high congruence among organization components and strategy can inhibit organizational change.

15.9 [p. 291] (T)
The need to innovate is one motivation for joint ventures and alliances.

15.10 [p. 285] (the people in the organization)
Levi Strauss has a well defined set of values organized around two dimensions--a commitment to social values and a commitment to _____.

15.11 [p. 289] (T)
The hit industry typology includes drillers, pumpers, and distributors.

15.12 [p. 292] (F)
Kaizen means to start from a clean sheet of paper and to search for and implement radical change to achieve breakthrough results.

15.13 [p. 278] (systems and culture)
The four constructs that are at the core of the framework for analyzing organizations are people, structure, _____ and _____.

15.14 [p. 285] (T)
An organizational culture provides the key to strategy implementation because it is such a powerful force for providing focus, motivation, and norms.

15.15 [p. 277] (T)
The assessment of any strategy should include a careful analysis of organizational risks and a judgment about the nature of any required organizational changes and their associated costs and feasibility.

15.16 [p. 278] (B)
Four key constructs that describe the organization include all but one of the following:
        (a) people
        (b) competitor's commitment
        (c) systems
        (d) culture
        (e) structure

15.17 [p. 287] (D)
An organization's culture involves all but one of the following:
      (a) symbolic actions
      (b) shared values
      (c) norms of behavior
      (d) political party affiliation
      (e) symbols

16.1 [p. 297] (T)
Studies suggest that the performance of firms using formal planning systems is superior to that of those not using such systems.

16.2 [p. 297] (F)
The function of a planning staff should be to create strategies.

16.3 [p. 299] (F)
A formal planning system should be driven by a spreadsheet structure and should emerge with a plan that is summarized by a spreadsheet.

16.4 [p. 301] (T)
A key element of the planning system of SHV, the Dutch multinational, was the fact that all SBUs did not get reviewed in the same level of detail.

16.5 [p. 300] (T)
One pitfall of a formal planning process is to generate plans without "soul."

16.6 [p. 300] (plans that are too rigid and detailed, restricting planning to the annual cycle)
The pitfalls of a formal planning process include the dominance of short-term objectives, lack of commitment to the process outputs, the spreadsheet-driven process, _____, and _____.

16.7 [p. 294] (T)
Strategy development requires systematic and structured information gathering, a willingness to consider new directions, managerial insight, and an ability to think strategically.

16.8 [p. 300] (A)

Some of the pitfalls of the planning process include all but one of the following:

    (a) flexible plans

    (b) spreadsheet mode

    (c) annual cycle constraints

    (d) focus on short-term financials

    (e) plans without soul

SECTION 15

CHANGES IN THE FIFTH EDITION

Three changes should be called to the attention of those who have used prior editions of *Strategic Market Management*.

First, the strategic question construct has been changed to strategic uncertainty. This construct plays a central role in our teaching of the material. It proved to be impossible for people to interpret strategic question as uncertainly—they always wanted to include a strategic decision as a strategic question. Hopefully, the name change will help.

Second, another key construct, assets and skills, is now assets and competencies. The term *competencies* has been made popular by Hamel and Prahalad. In my view, core competencies excludes assets and thus I have chosen the phrase assets and competencies even though it is a bit bulky.

Third, the chapter on portfolio analysis has been compressed and put into the prior chapter, Chapter 7 - Internal Analysis.

There have been extensive revisions and updates throughout. The following are worth calling to the attention of users of prior editions:

Chapter 1: Introduction
Material from Hamel and Prahalad's "Competing for the Future" has been added.

Chapter 2: Overview
Added the Baskin-Robbins case study. The material on business mission has been replaced with new material on a business vision from Collins and Porras.

Chapter 4: Competitor Analysis
New material on expanding the radar screen from Slywotzky has been added.

Chapter 5: Market Analysis
The CD industry is used as a case study of excessive capacity and cross channel price problems. Added growth submarkets. Updated trends section.

Chapter 6: Environmental Analysis
The chapter is now divided in half. The second half is "Dealing with Strategic Uncertainly" and covers impact analysis and scenario analysis.

Chapter 7: Internal Analysis

A condensed business portfolio analysis is now a part of this chapter.

Chapter 8: SCA

The concept of a paradigm shift under strategic stubbornness is elaborated . Strategy as revolution material from Hamel is added.

Chapter 9: Differentiation

The brand equity material is rewritten drawing from Aaker's *Building Strong Brands*.

Chapter 10: Low Cost, Focus, Pre-emptive Move

The Procter & Gamble cost leadership story has been added. A section on first-mover advantage in high tech industries has been added. A study on early market leaders by Golder and Tellis is reported.

Chapter 12: Diversification

The brand extension material has been updated.

Chapter 15: Implementation

Mintzberg's "easy steps to destroy real value" has been added.

Chapter 16: Formal Planning Systems

The EDS story of creating the future as told by Hamel and Prahalad is told.

Appendix

The example setting is Pet Food, which has been updated.

SECTION 16

POWERPOINT PRESENTATIONS BY CHAPTER

Chapter 1

Business Strategy:

The Concept and Trends in Its Management

"Plans are nothing, planning is everything"

- Dwight D. Eisenhower

"Where absolute superiority is not attainable, you must produce a relative one at the decisive point by making skillful use of what you have."

- Karl von Clauseweitz

What is a Business Strategy?

- Product Market

- Investment

- Functional Area Strategies

- Strategic Assets or Competencies

- Allocation of Resources

- Synergy across Businesses

A Business Strategy

Basis of SCAs
- Assets/Competencies
- Synergies

The Product-Market Investment Decision
- Product-market scope
- Investment intensity
- Resource allocation

Functional Area Strategies
- Product
- Price
- Distribution
- Etc.

Figure 1.1

Strategic Thrusts
- The Search for an SCA

Differentiation

Low Cost

Focus

Preemptive Move

Synergy

Characteristics and Trends

- External, Market Orientation
- Proactive Strategies
- Importance of Information Systems
- On-Line Analysis and Decision Making
- Entrepreneurial Thrust

- Implementation
- Global Realities
- Longer Time Horizon
- Empirical Research
- Interdisiplinary Developments

Why Strategic Market Management?

- Precipitate consideration of strategic choices

- Force long-range view

- Make visible resource allocation decisions

- Aid strategic analysis and decision making

- Provide a strategic management and control system

- Provide horizontal and vertical communication and coordination systems

- Cope with change

Chapter 2

Strategic Market Management:

An Overview

"Chance favors the prepared mind."

- Louis Pasteur

"Far better an approximate answer to the right question, which is often vague, than an exact answer to the wrong question, which can always be made precise."

- John Tukey, statistician

"If you don't know where you are going, you might end up somewhere else."

— *Casey Stengel*

Overview

External Analysis
- Customer Analysis
- Competitor Analysis
- Market Analysis
- Environmental Analysis

Internal Analysis
- Performance Analysis
- Determinants of Strategic option

Strategy Identification and Selection

Figure 2.1

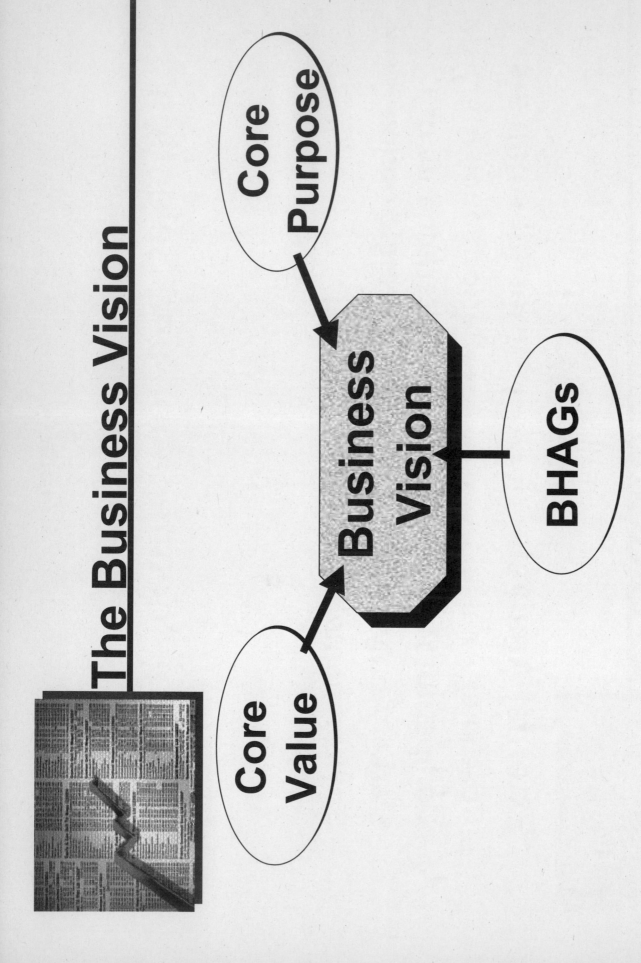

The Business Vision

Core Purpose

Core Value

Business Vision

BHAGs

Figure 2.2

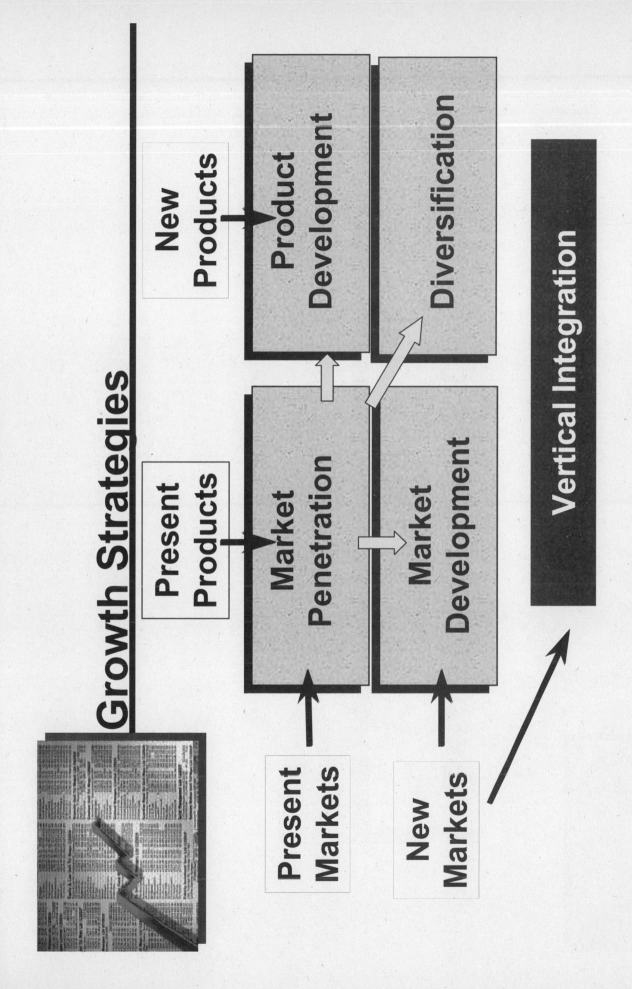

Growth Strategies

	Present Products	New Products
Present Markets	Market Penetration	Product Development
New Markets	Market Development	Diversification

Vertical Integration

Source: H. Igor Ansoff, "Strategic Diversification", Harvard Business Review, September-October 1957, pp.113-24

2-7

Figure 2.4

Chapter 3

External Analysis Overview and Customer Analysis

"The purpose of an enterprise is to create and keep a customer."

- Theodore Leavitt

"Consumers are statistics.
Customers are people."

- *Stanley Marcus*

The Role of External Analysis

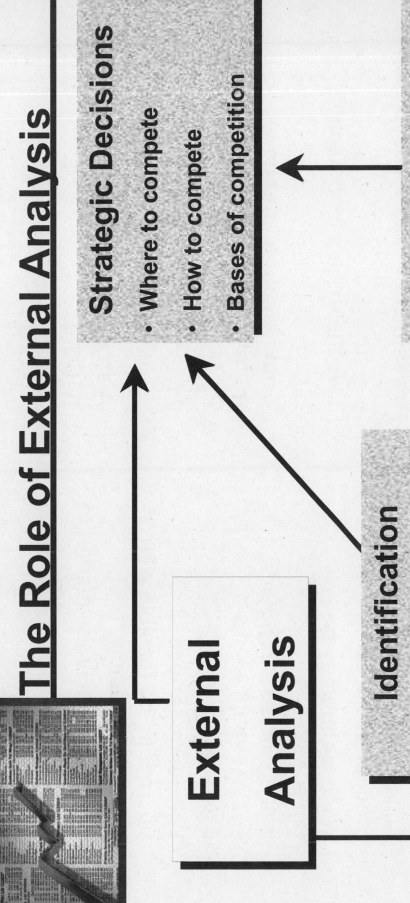

External Analysis

Strategic Decisions
- Where to compete
- How to compete
- Bases of competition

Identification
- Trends/future events
- Threats/opportunities
- Strategic uncertainties

Analysis
- Information-need areas
- Scenario analysis

Figure 3.1

Strategic Uncertainties

Strategic Uncertainties

- Will a major firm enter?
- Will a tofu-based dessert product be accepted?
- Will a technology be replaced?
- Will the dollar strengthen against an off-shore currency?
- Will computer-based operations be feasible with current technology?
- How sensitive is the market to price?

Strategic Decisions

- Investment in a product market
- Investment in a tofu-based product
- Investment in a technology
- Commitment to off-shore manufacturing
- Investment in a new system
- A strategy of maintaining price parity

The Loyalty Matrix: Priorities

	Switchers	Fence Sitters	Loyal
Customer	Medium	High	Highest
Non-customer	Low to medium	High	Low

Figure 3.4

Segmentation

How should segments be defined?

- *Benefit Segmentation*

- *Price Sensitivity*

- *Loyalty*

- *Application Segmentation*

- *Multiple Segment versus Focus Strategy*

Customer Motivation Analysis

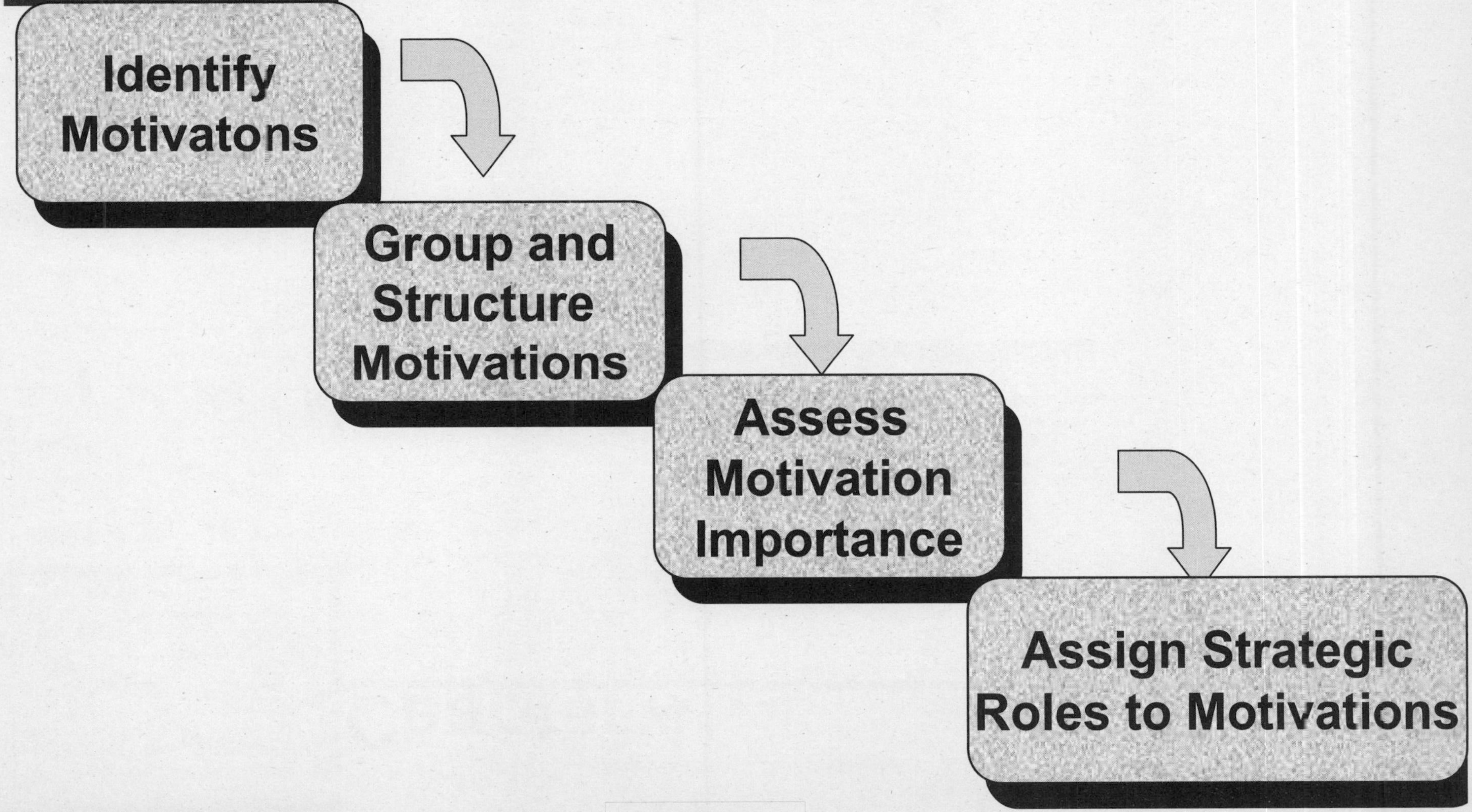

Identify Motivatons

Group and Structure Motivations

Assess Motivation Importance

Assign Strategic Roles to Motivations

Figure 3.6

Chapter 4

Competitor Analysis

"Induce your competitors not to invest in those products, markets and services where you expect to invest the most...that is the fundamental role of strategy."

- Bruce Henderson
Founder of BCG

"There is nothing more exhilarating than to be shot at without result."

- Winston Churchill

Competitor Analysis

Strategic Groups

– *Pursue similar competitive strategies*

– *Have similar characteristics*

– *Have similar assets and competencies*

Competitor Analysis

Potential Competitors

- *Market expansion*
- *Product expansion*
- *Backward integration*
- *Forward integration*
- *Export assets or competencies*
- *Retaliatory or defensive strategies*

Understanding the Competitors

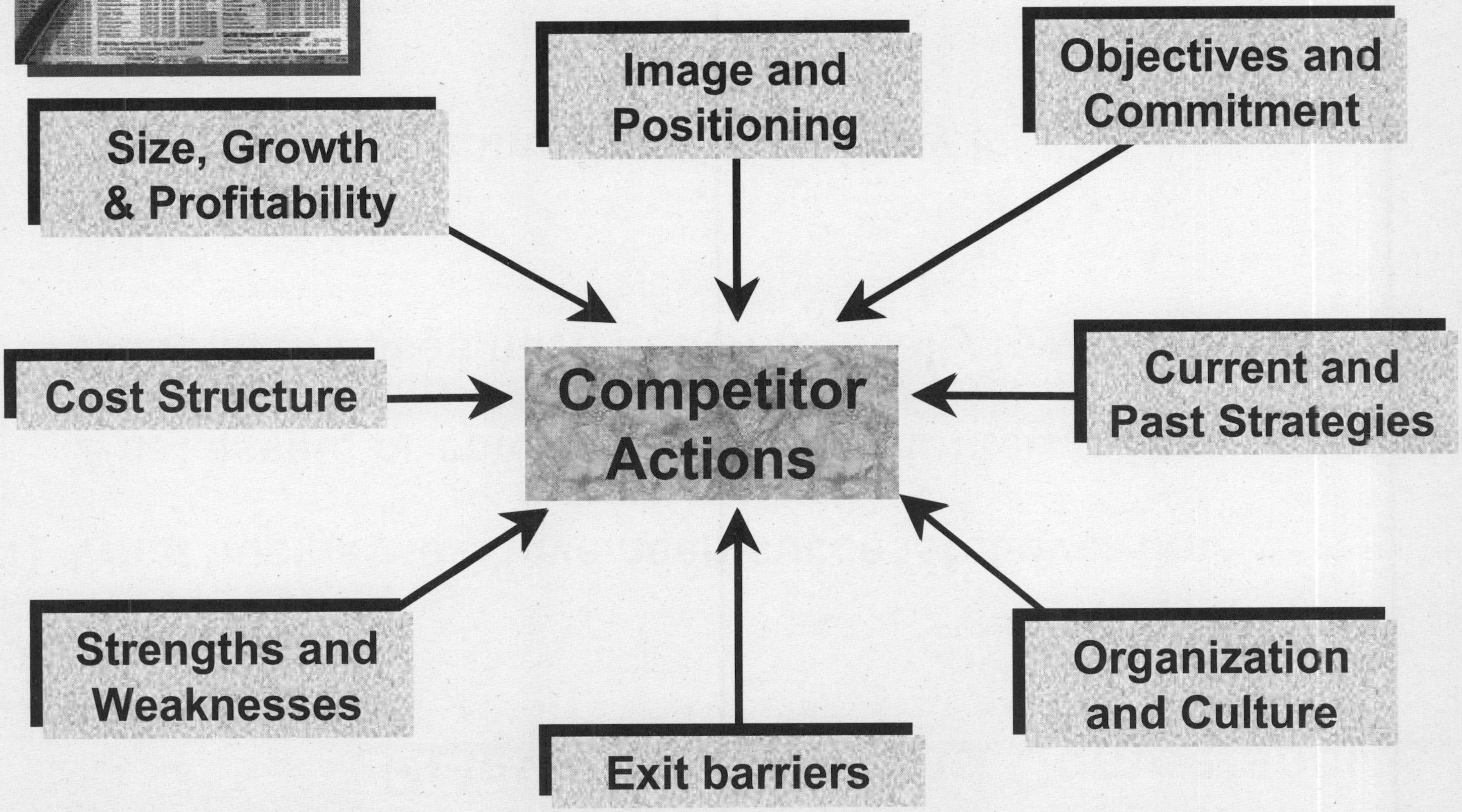

Objectives and Commitment

Current and Past Strategies

Organization and Culture

Image and Positioning

Competitor Actions

Exit barriers

Size, Growth & Profitability

Cost Structure

Strengths and Weaknesses

Figure 4.3

Relevant Assets and Competencies

1) What businesses have been successful over time?

What assets or competencies contributed to their success?

What businesses have had chronically low performance?

Why?

What assets or competencies do they lack?

Relevant Assets and Competencies

2) What are the key customer motivations?

What is really important to the customer?

3) What are the large value-added parts of the product or service?

What are the large cost components?

Relevant Assets and Competencies

4) What are the mobility barriers in the industry?

5) Consider the components of the value chain. Do any provide the potential to generate a competitive advantage?

The Value Chain

Margin

Margin

Firm Infrastructure

Human Resource Management

Technology Development

Procurement

Support Activities

Inbound Logistics

Operations

Outbound Logistics

Marketing & Sales

Service

Primary Activities

Source: Reprinted with permission © 1985 Michae Porter 4-10

Figure 4.5

Chapter 5

Market Analysis

"As the economy, led by the automobile industry, rose to a new high level in the twenties, a complex of new elements came into existence to transform the market: installment selling, the used-car trade-in, the closed body, and the annual model. (I would add improved roads if I were to take into account the environment of the automobile.)"

- Alfred P. Slaon, Jr., General Motors

"Imagining the future may be more important than analyzing the past. I daresay companies today are not resource-bound, they are imagination-bound."

- C.K. Prahalad
University of Michigan

Dimensions of Market Analysis

- Actual and potential market size

- Market growth

- Market profitability

- Cost structure

- Distribution systems

- Trends and developments

- Key success factors

Detecting Maturity and Decline

- Price pressure

- Buyer sophistication and knowledge

- Substitute products or technologies

- Saturation

- No growth sources

- Customer disinterest

Porter's Five-Factor Model

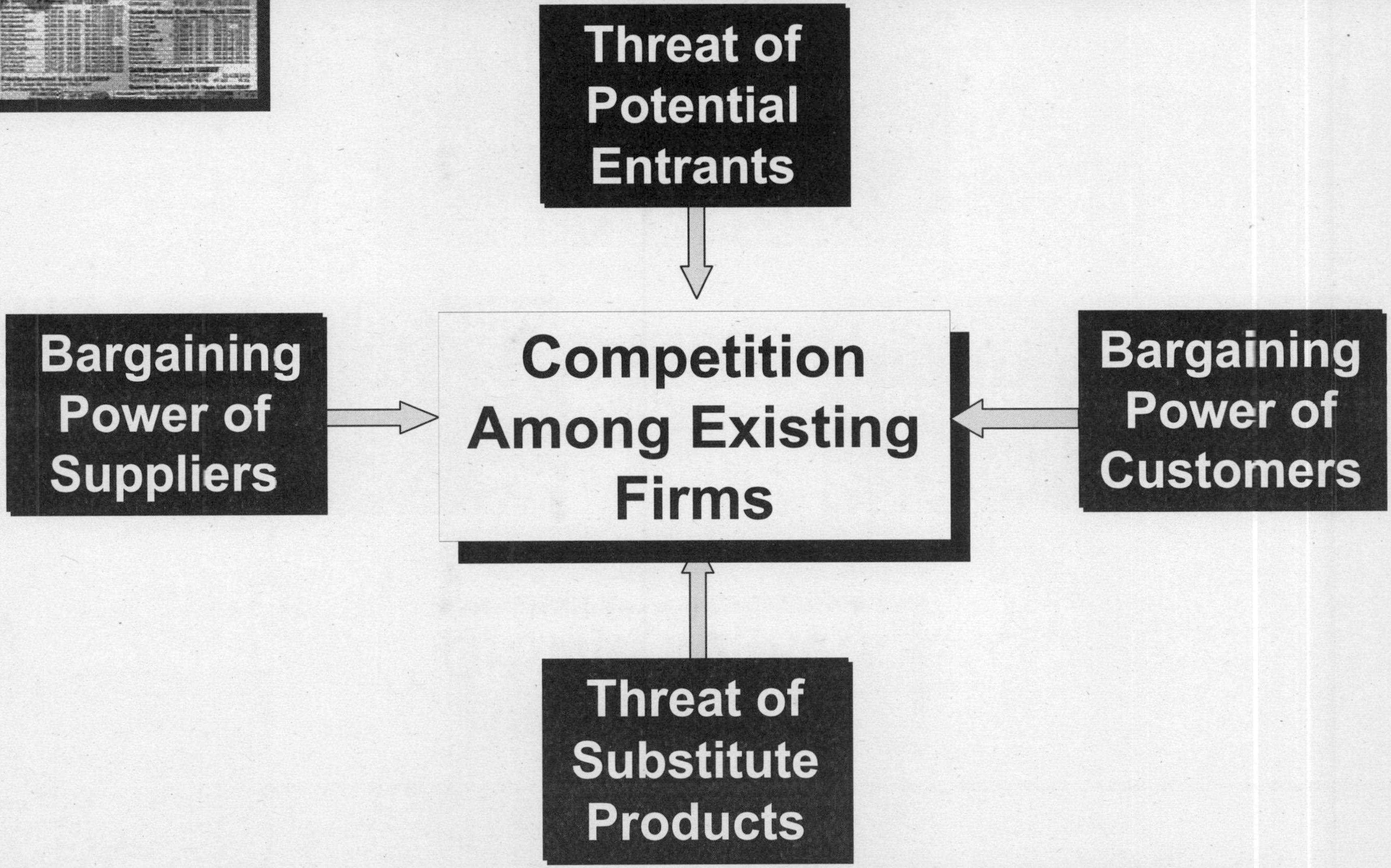

Threat of Potential Entrants

Bargaining Power of Customers

Competition Among Existing Firms

Bargaining Power of Suppliers

Threat of Substitute Products

Source: Adapted from Michael E. Porter, "Industry Structure and Competitive Strategy: Keys to Profitability" Financial Analysis Journal, July-August 1980, p.33.

Figure 5.3

Risks of High-Growth Markets

Firm Limitations
- Resource constraints
- Distribution unavailable

Competitive Risk
- Overcrowding
- Superior competitive entry

Market Changes
- Changing KSFs
- New technology
- Disappointing growth
- Price instability

Figure 5.5

Chapter 6

Environmental Analysis and Dealing with Strategic Uncertainty

"There is something in the wind."

- William Shakespeare
The Comedy of Errors

"A poorly observed fact is more treacherous than a faulty train of reasoning."

- Paul Valéry,
French Philosopher

Dimensions of Environmental Analysis

- **Technology**
  - Impact of new technologies
  - Forecasting new technologies
- **Government**
- **Economics**
- **Culture**
- **Demographics**

Forecasting Environmental Trends and Events

- Asking the Right Questions

- Trend Extrapolation

- Asking Experts

- Decomposing the Task

- Cross-Impact Analysis

Strategic Uncertainties Categories

Immediacy

	Low	**High**
High	Monitor and analyze; contingent strategies considered	In-depth analysis; develop strategy
Low	Monitor	Monitor and analyze

Impact

Figure 6.2

Scenario Analysis

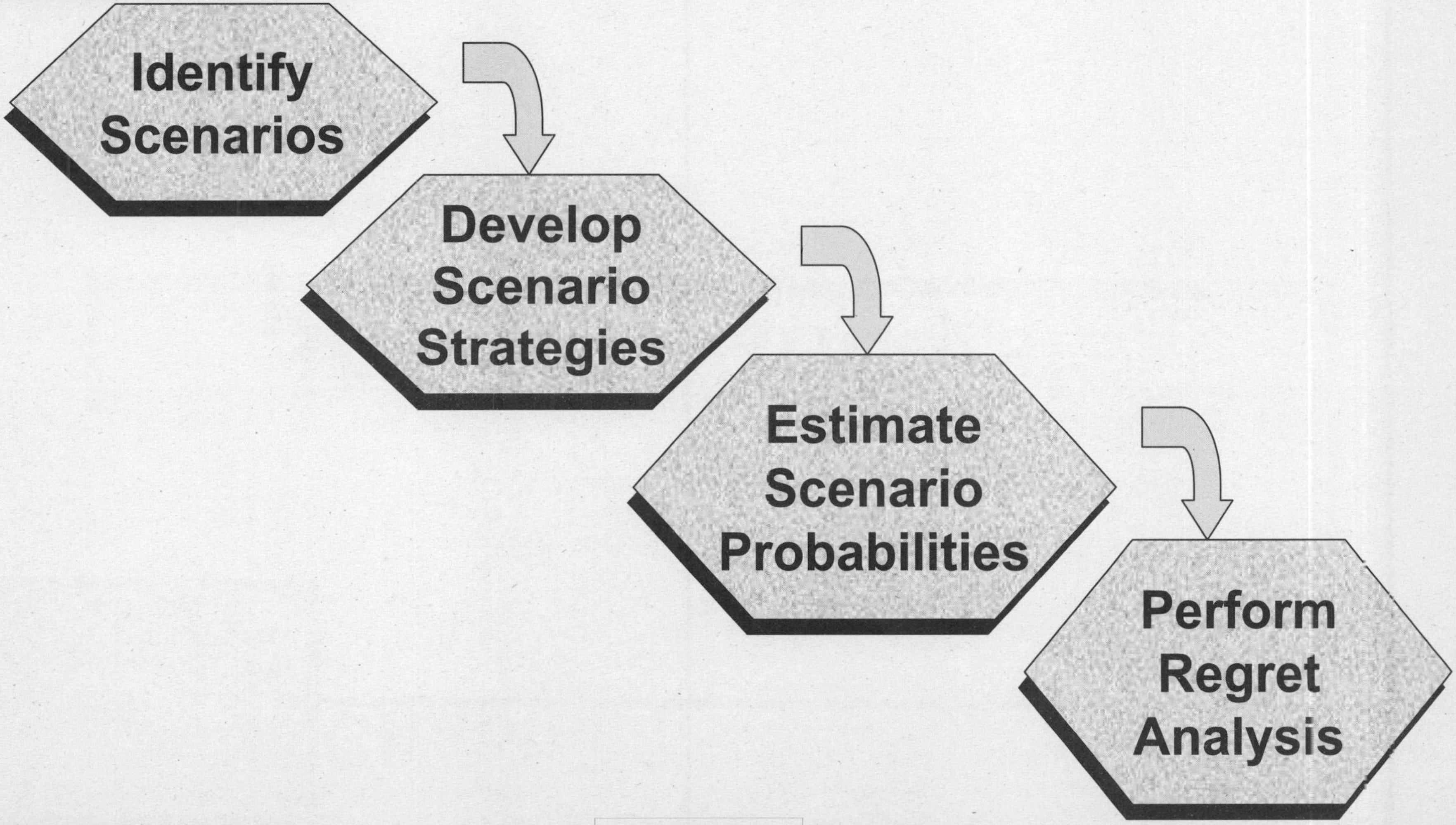

Identify Scenarios → Develop Scenario Strategies → Estimate Scenario Probabilities → Perform Regret Analysis

Figure 6.3

Chapter 7

Internal Analysis

"We have met the enemy and he is us."

- *Pogo*

"Self-conceit may lead to self-destruction."

- Aesop

"The Frog and the Ox"

"The fish is last to know if it swims in water."

- *Chinese proverb*

Performance Measures Reflecting Long-Term Profitability

Customer Satisfaction/ Brand Loyalty

Product/Service Quality

Brand/Firm Associations

Relative Cost

New Product Activity

Manager/employee Capability and Performance

Current Performance

Long Term Profits

Figure 7.1

Relative Cost vs. Relative Performance - Strategic Implications

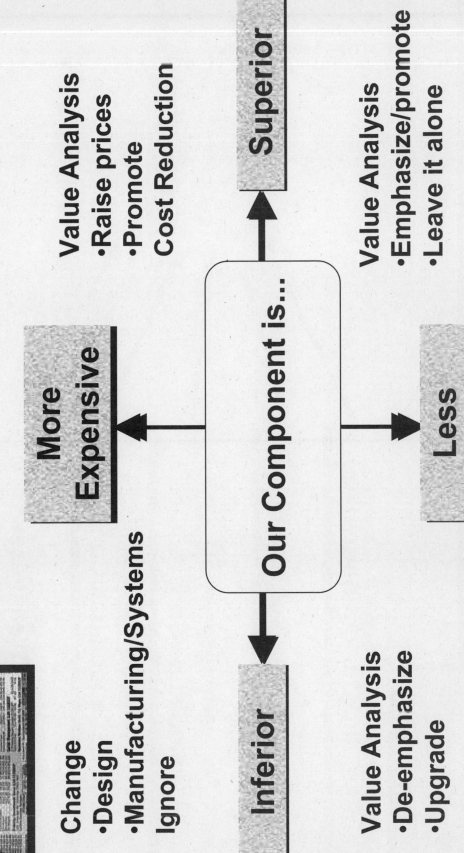

Value Analysis
- Raise prices
- Promote
- Cost Reduction

More Expensive

Change
- Design
- Manufacturing/Systems
- Ignore

Our Component is...

Superior

Value Analysis
- Emphasize/promote
- Leave it alone

Less Expensive

Inferior

Value Analysis
- De-emphasize
- Upgrade

Figure 7.2

Determinants of
Strategic Options and Choices

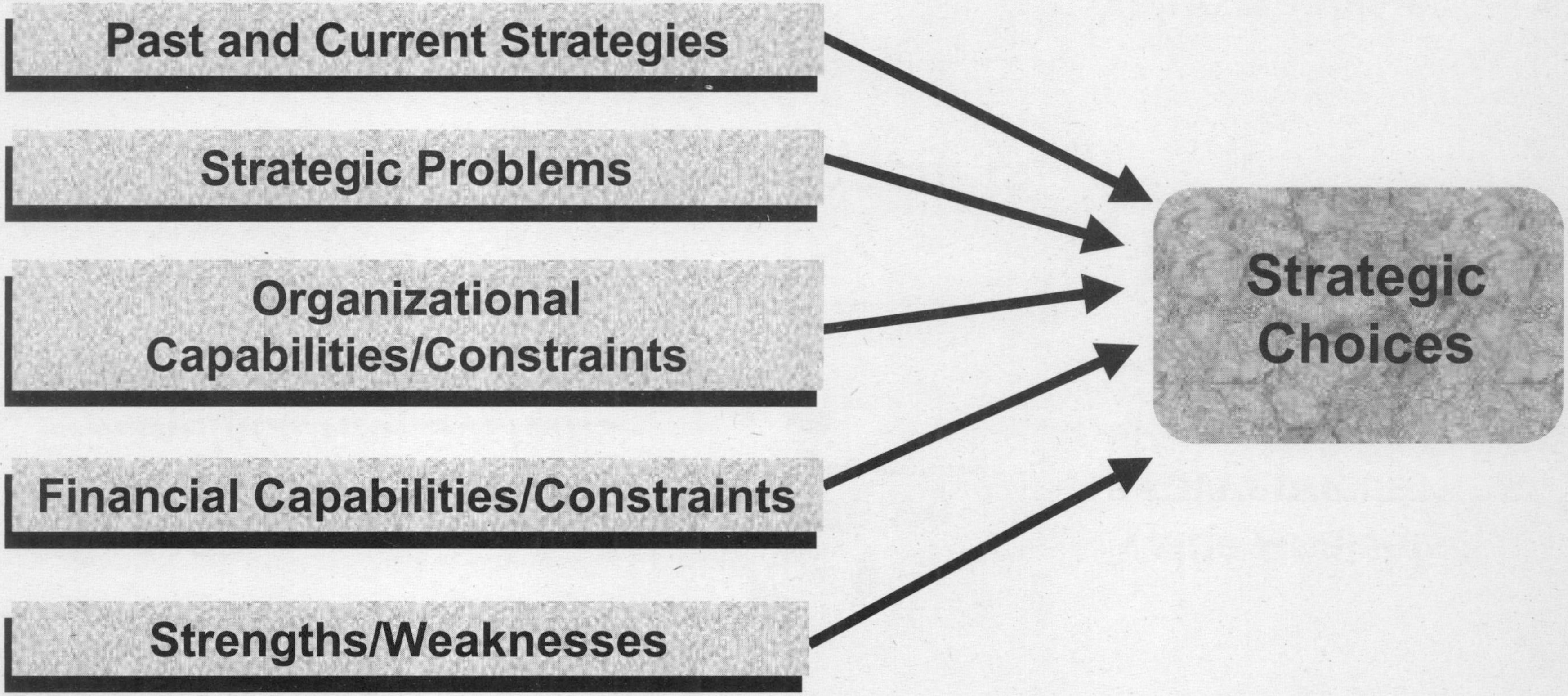

Strategic Choices

- Past and Current Strategies
- Strategic Problems
- Organizational Capabilities/Constraints
- Financial Capabilities/Constraints
- Strengths/Weaknesses

Figure 7.3

Structuring Strategic Decisions

Competitor Strengths and Weaknesses

Organizational Strengths and Weaknesses

Strategic Decision
- Strategic Investment
- Functional Strategy Areas
- Sustainable Competitive Advantage

Market Needs, Attractiveness, and Key Success Factors

Figure 7.4

The Market Attractiveness-Business Position Matrix

Market Attractiveness

	High	Medium	Low

Business Position

High

Medium

Low

Invest/ Grow

Selective Investment

Harvest/ Divest

Figure 7.5

Evaluating Ability to Compete

- Size
- Growth
- Share by segment
- Customer loyalty
- Margins
- Distribution

- Technology skills
- Patents
- Marketing
- Flexibility
- Organization

Evaluating Market Attractiveness

- Size
- Growth
- Customer
  Satisfaction levels
- Competition:
  quantity, types,
  effectiveness,
  commitment

- Price levels
- Profitability
- Technology
- Governmental
  regulations
- Sensitivity to economic
  trends

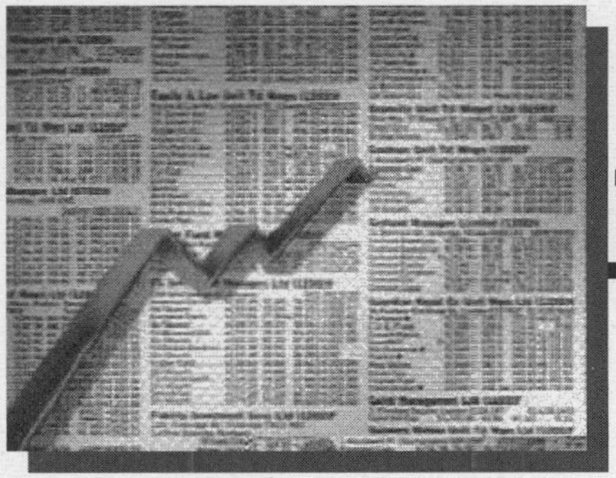

The Growth-Share Matrix

	High	Low
High	Stars	Problem Children
Low	Cash Cows	Dogs

Market Growth Rate

Competitive Position

Figure 7.6

Chapter 8

Obtaining A Sustainable Competitive Advantage

"Vision is the art of seeing things invisible."

- Jonathan Swift

"All men can see the tactics whereby I conquer, but what none can see is the strategy out of which great victory is evolved."

- *Sun-Tzu*

Chinese Military Strategist

"Don't manage, lead."

- Jack Welch, GE

The Sustainable Competitive Advantage

The Way You Compete
- Product Strategy
- Positioning Strategy
- Manufacturing Strategy
- Distribution Strategy, etc.

Basis of Competition
- Assets and Competencies

Where You Compete
- Product-market Selection

Whom You Compete Against
- Competitor Selection

SCA

Figure 8.1

Characteristics of SCAs

- Substantial

- Sustainable

- Leveraged

Strategic Thrusts

Differentiation

Low Cost

Focus

Preemptive Move

Synergy

Figure 8.3

Strategic Vision

- A clear future strategy

- Buy-in throughout the organization

- Assets, competencies, and resources

- Patience

Vision versus Opportunism

Strategic Approach	Strategic Risk
Strategic Vision	**Strategic Stubbornness**
Strategic Opportunism	**Strategic Drift**

Focus on Future
Focus on Present

Figure 8.5

Strategic Intent

- Captures essence of winning

- Is stable over time

- Sets target that deserves personal effort and commitment

- Implies sizeable stretch

Chapter 9

Differentiation Strategies

"Ever since Morton's put a little girl in a yellow slicker and declared, 'When it rains, it pours,' no advertising person worth his or her salt has had any excuse to think of a product as having parity with anything."

- Malcom MacDougal
Jordan Case McGrath

"If you don't have a competitive advantage, don't compete"

— *Jack Welch,*
GE

"The secret of success is constancy to purpose."

- Benjamin Disraeli

A successful differentiation strategy should

Be Difficult to Copy

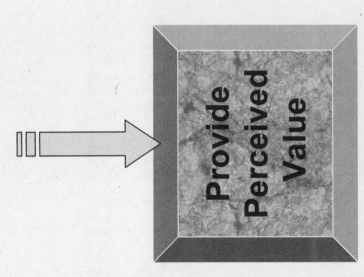

Provide Perceived Value

Generate Customer Value

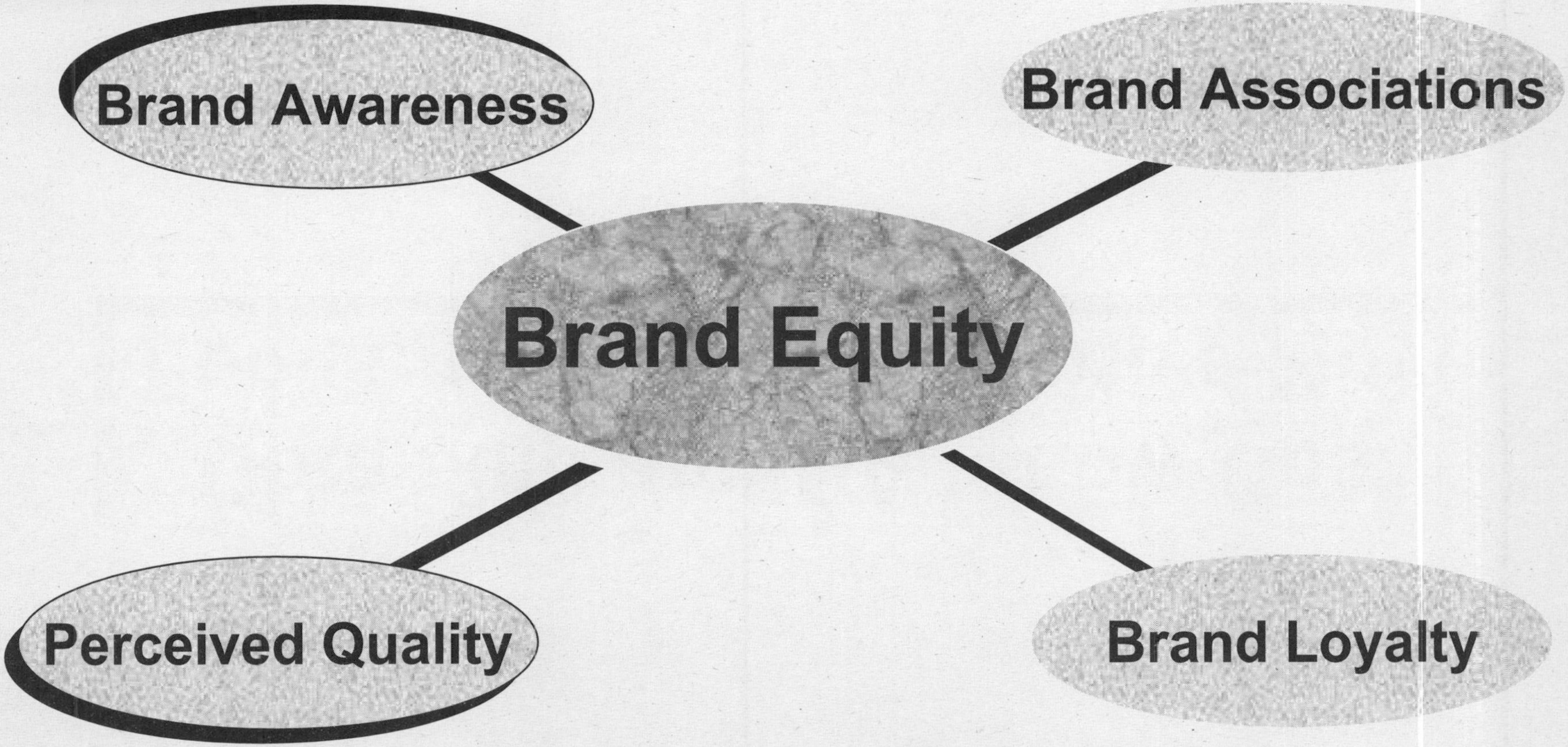

Brand Associations

Brand Loyalty

Brand Equity

Brand Awareness

Perceived Quality

Figure 9.3

Chapter 10

Obtaining an SCA — Low Cost, Focus, and The Preemptive Move

"Never follow the crowd."

- Bernard M. Baruch

"The first man gets the oyster, the second man gets the shell."

- Andrew Carnegie

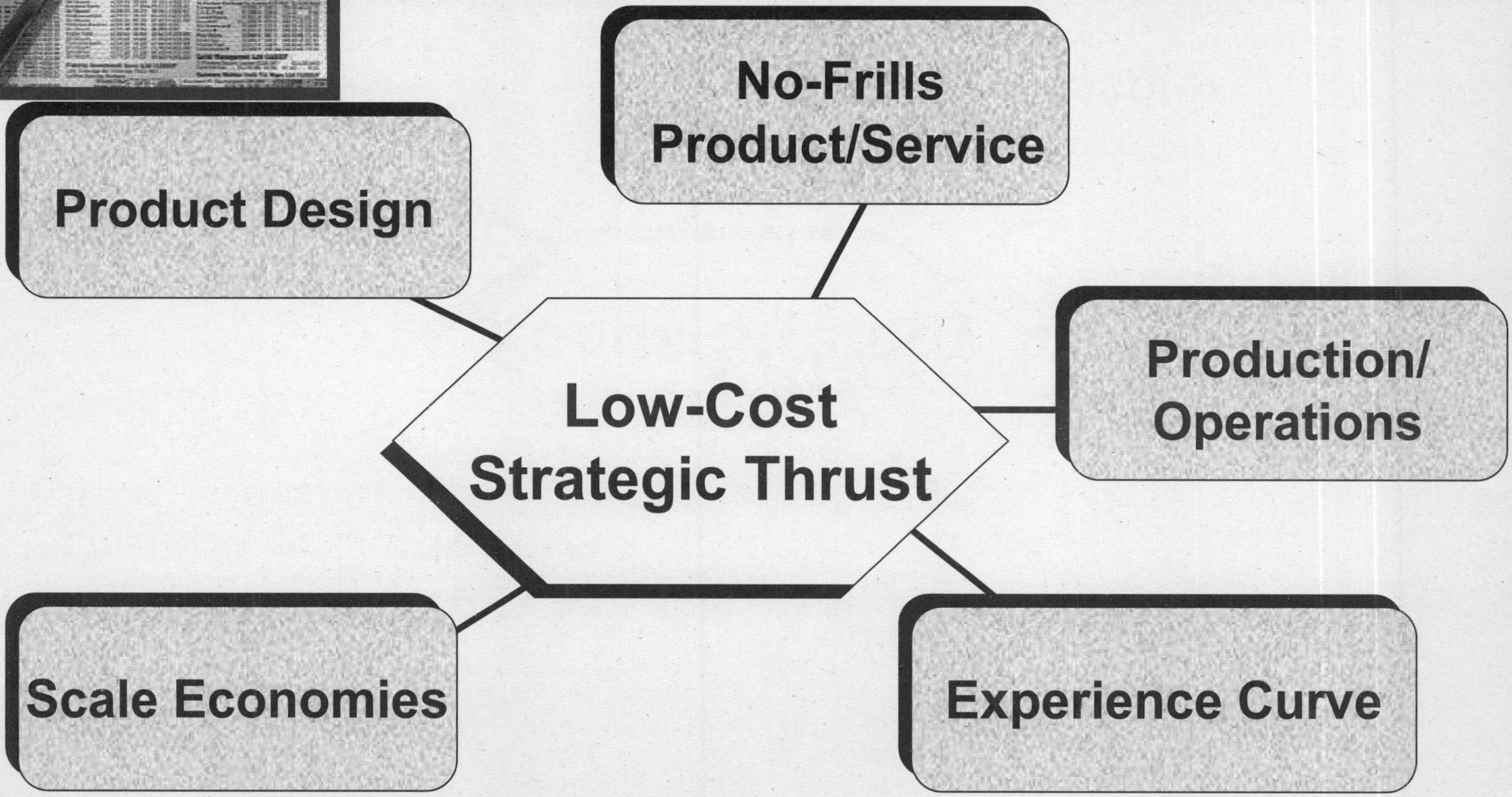

Low-Cost Strategic Thrust

- No-Frills Product/Service
- Production/Operations
- Experience Curve
- Product Design
- Scale Economies

Figure 10.1

Focus Strategy

Compete with Limited Resources

Providing Positioning Strategy

Bypass Competitor Assets/Competencies

Avoid Strategy Dilution or Distraction

Reduce Competitive Pressures

Figure 10.4

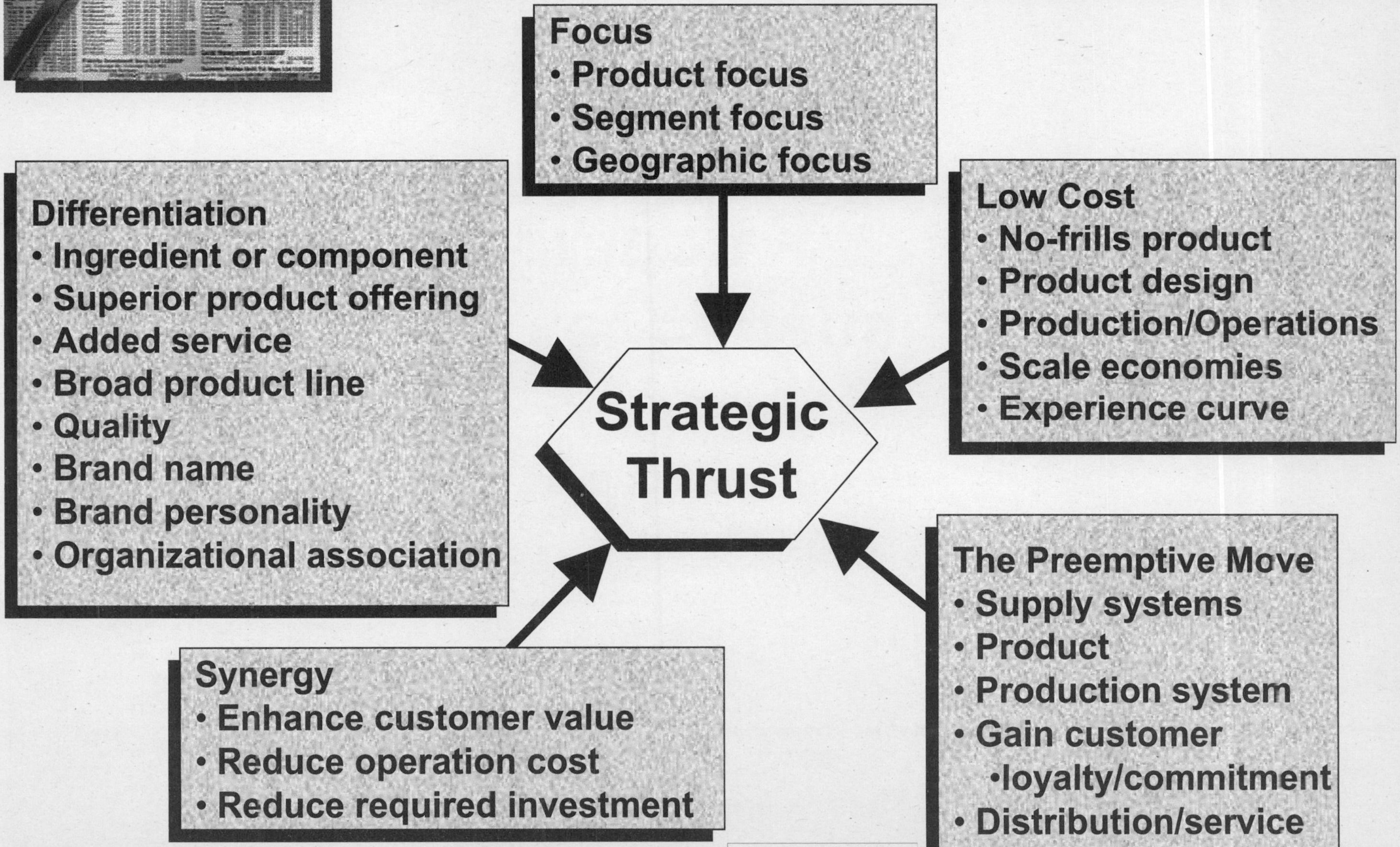

Focus
- Product focus
- Segment focus
- Geographic focus

Low Cost
- No-frills product
- Product design
- Production/Operations
- Scale economies
- Experience curve

The Preemptive Move
- Supply systems
- Product
- Production system
- Gain customer
- loyalty/commitment
- Distribution/service

Differentiation
- Ingredient or component
- Superior product offering
- Added service
- Broad product line
- Quality
- Brand name
- Brand personality
- Organizational association

Synergy
- Enhance customer value
- Reduce operation cost
- Reduce required investment

Strategic Thrust

Figure 10.6

Chapter 11

Growth Strategies: Penetration, Product-Market Expansion, and Vertical Integration

"Marketing should focus on market creation, not market sharing."

- Regis McKenna

"Results are gained by exploiting opportunities, not by solving problems."

- *Peter Drucker*

Alternative Growth Strategies

	Present Products	New Products

Present Markets	**I. Growth in existing product markets**
	• Increase market share
	• Increase product usage
	  • Increase the frequency used
	  • Increase the quantity used
	  • Find new applications for current users
		II. Product Development
		• Add product features, product refinement
		• Expand the product line
		• Develop a new generation product
		• Develop new products for same market

New Markets	**III. Market Development** • Expand geographically • Target new segments	**V. Diversification involving new products and new markets** • Related • Unrelated

Vertical Integration

IV. Vertical Integration Strategies
• Forward integration
• Backward integration

Figure 11.1

Chapter 12

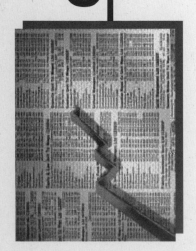

Diversification

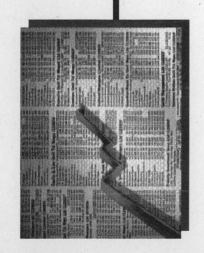

"Tis the part of a wiseman to keep himself today for tomorrow, and not venture all his eggs in one basket."

- *Miguel de Cervantes*

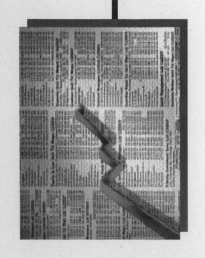

"Put all your eggs in one basket
and — WATCH THAT BASKET."
          - *Mark Twain*

Positive Attribute Associations

Perceived Quality Associations

Brand Name

Negative Attribute Associations

Product Class Associations

12-4

Figure 12.1

© 1999 John Wiley & Sons

Chapter 13

Strategies in Declining and Hostile Markets

"Anyone can hold the helm when the sea is calm."

- Publilius Syrus

"Where there is no wind, row."

- Portuguese proverb

Revitalizing a Stagnant Market

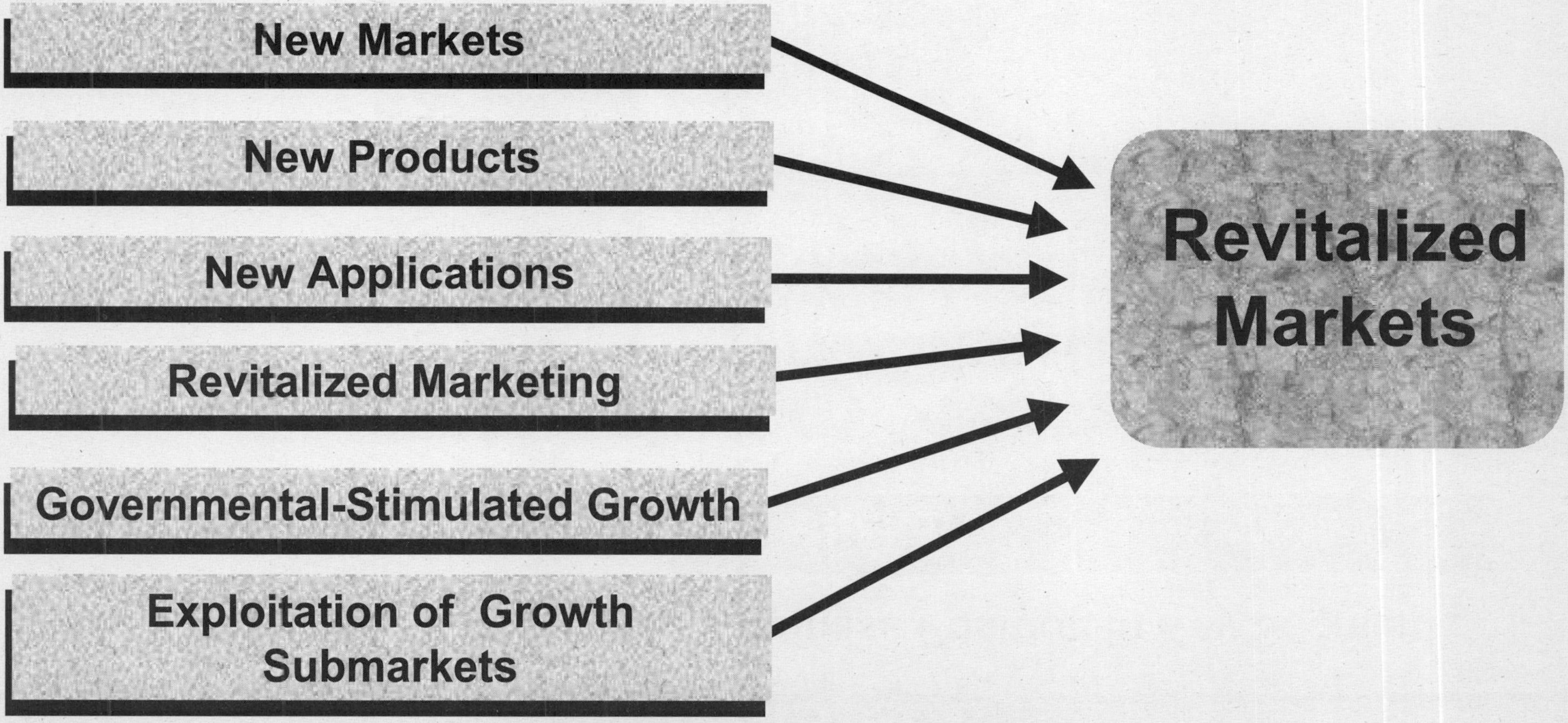

Revitalized Markets

- New Markets
- New Products
- New Applications
- Revitalized Marketing
- Governmental-Stimulated Growth
- Exploitation of Growth Submarkets

Figure 13.1

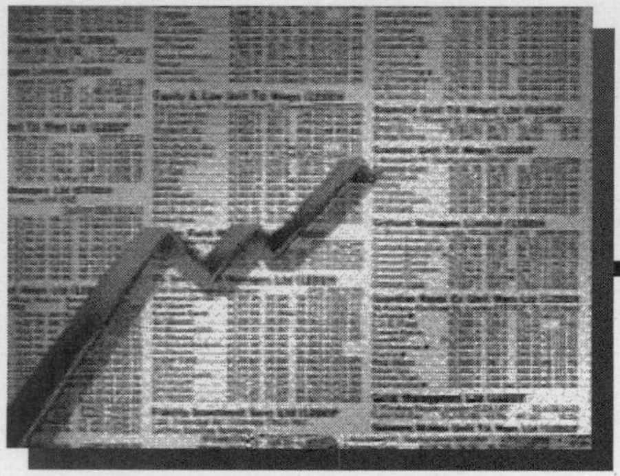

Strategies for Declining or Stagnant Industries

Business Position in Key Segments

	Strong	Weak
Favorable	Invest or hold	Milk or exit
Unfavorable	Milk or exit	Exit

Industry Environment

Figure 13.2

The Investment Decision in a Declining Industry

Some Strategic Uncertainties

- Market Prospects
- Competitive Intensity
- Performance/Strengths
- Interrelationships With Other Businesses
- Implementation Barriers

Figure 13.3

Six Phases of Hostility

- Phase 1 - Margin pressure

- Phase 2 - Share shifts

- Phase 3 - Product proliferation

- Phase 4 - Self-defeating cost reduction

- Phase 5 - Consolidation and shakeout

- Phase 6 - Rescue

Figure 13.4

Chapter 14

Global Strategies

"Most managers are nearsighted. Even though today's competitive landscape often stretches to a global horizon, they see best what they know best: the customers geographically closest to home."

- Kenichi Ohmae

"A powerful force drives the world toward a converging commonality, and that force is technology... The result is a new commercial reality — the emergence of global markets for standardized consumer products on a previously unimagined scale of magnitude."

- *Theodore Levitt*

"My ventures are not in one bottom trusted, nor to one place."

- William Shakespeare
The Merchant of Venice

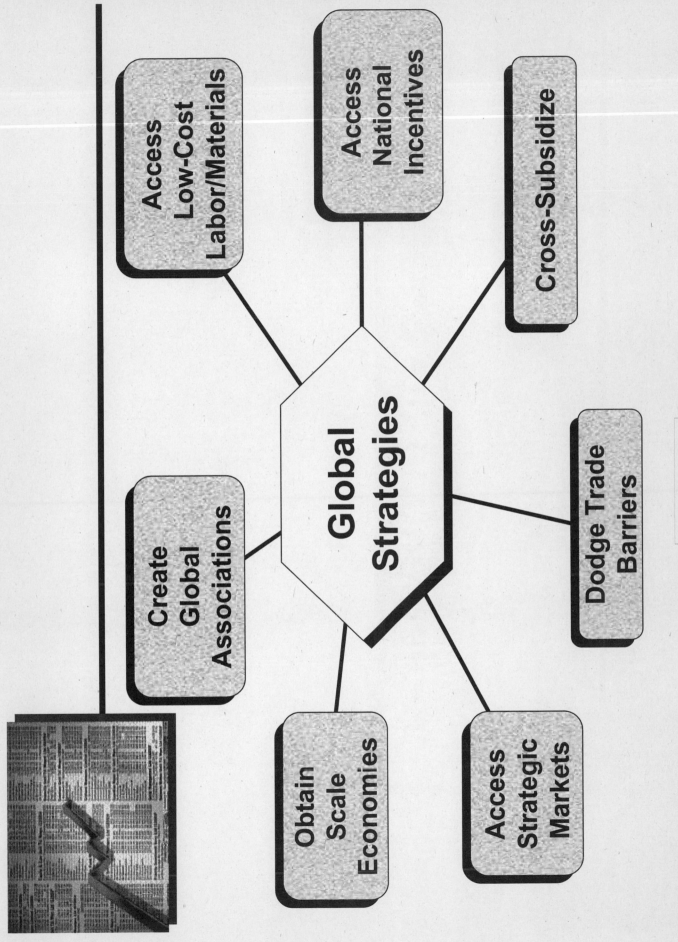

Access Low-Cost Labor/Materials

Access National Incentives

Cross-Subsidize

Create Global Associations

Global Strategies

Dodge Trade Barriers

Obtain Scale Economies

Access Strategic Markets

Figure 14.1

14-5

Chapter 15

Implementing the Strategy

"The basic philosophy, spirit and drive of an organization have far more to do with its relative achievements than do technological or economic resources, organizational structure, innovation and timing."

- *Thomas Watson, Jr,*
IBM

"Structure follows strategy."

- Alfred Chandler

"Never acquire a business you don't know how to run."

- Robert Johnson
Johnson & Johnson

A Framework for Analyzing Organizations

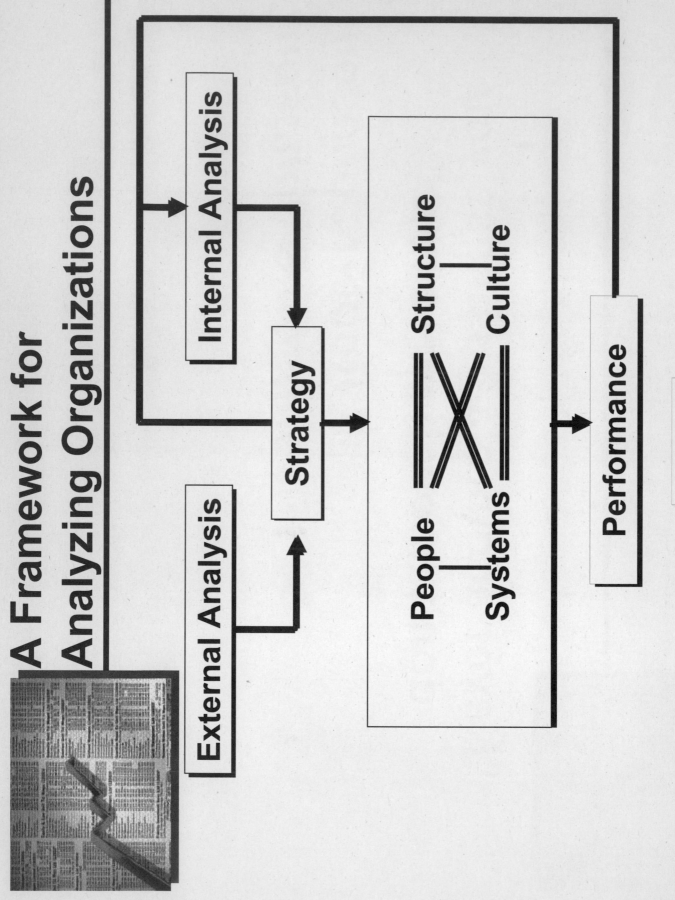

External Analysis

Internal Analysis

Strategy

People × Structure
Systems × Culture

Performance

Figure 15.1

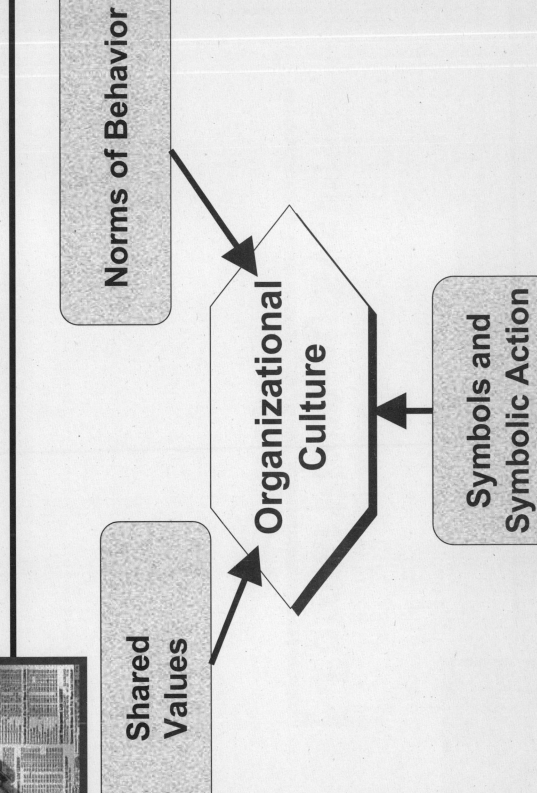

Norms of Behavior

Organizational Culture

Symbols and Symbolic Action

Shared Values

Figure 15.2

Chapter 16

Formal Planning Systems

"Strategic planning isn't strategic thinking. One is analysis and the other is synthesis."

- Henry Minztberg, McGill University

"Those that implement the plans must make the plans."

- Patrick Hagerty
Texas Instruments

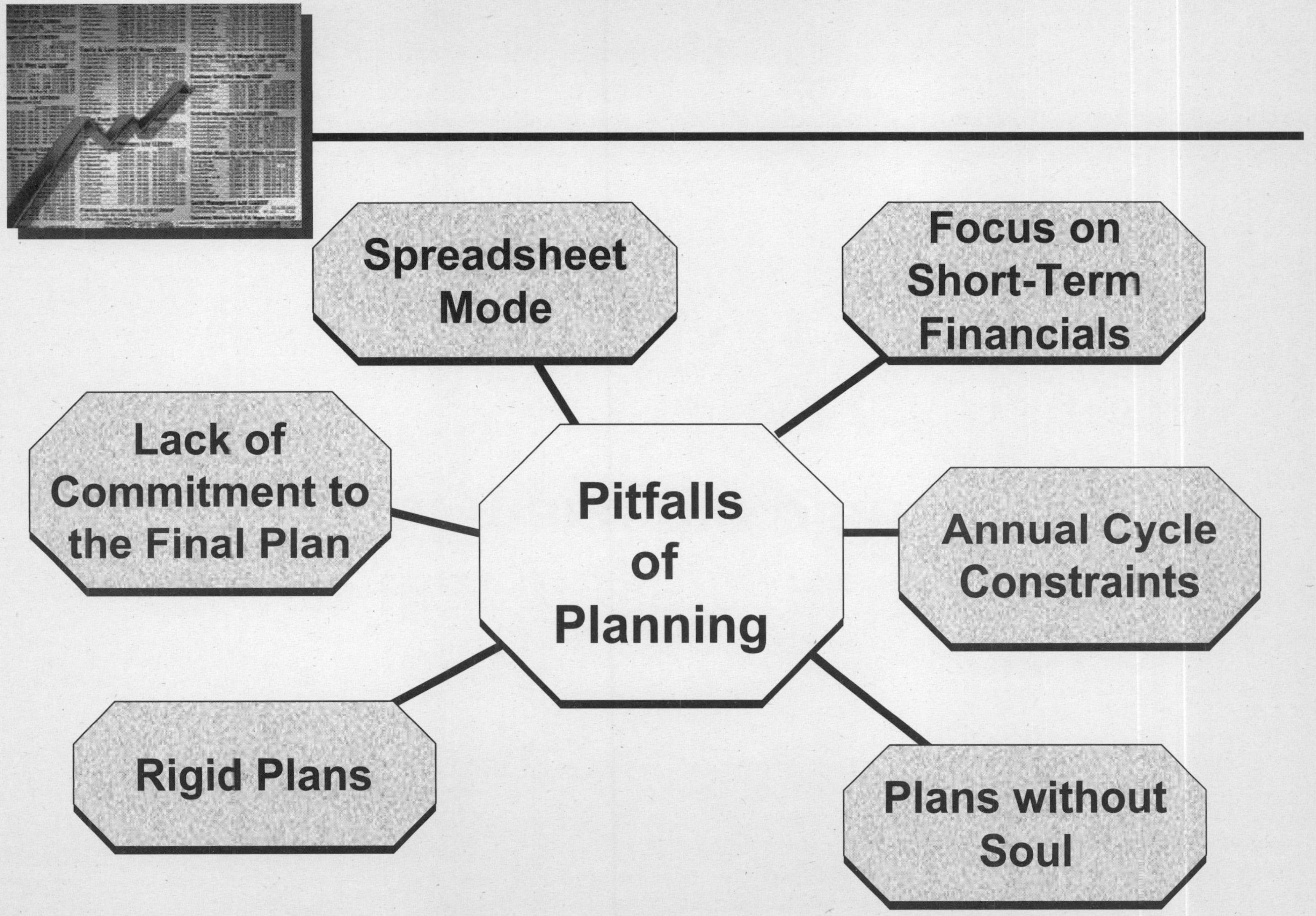

Focus on Short-Term Financials

Annual Cycle Constraints

Plans without Soul

Spreadsheet Mode

Pitfalls of Planning

Lack of Commitment to the Final Plan

Rigid Plans

Figure 16.2